BREAKING
the
CYCLE

BREAKING
the
CYCLE

Politics, Constitutional Change and Governance in St. Kitts and Nevis

Charles Wilkin QC

IAN RANDLE PUBLISHERS
Kingston • Miami

First published in Jamaica, 2015 by
Ian Randle Publishers
11 Cunningham Avenue
Box 686
Kingston 6
www.ianrandlepublishers.com

© Charles Wilkin
ISBN: 978-976-637-907-0

A CIP catalogue record for this book is available
from the National Library of Jamaica.

Cover and Book Design by Ian Randle Publishers
Printed and bound in the United States

Table of Contents

Preface

S t. Kitts and Nevis has been self-governing since February 27, 1967 and fully independent since September 19,1983. In its relatively short political history, the country has experienced a number of political crises, the latest of which is the subject of this book. What I describe as the 26-month election lasted from December 2012 until February 2015.

The book is divided into two parts.

In **Part One**, I describe the political events in St. Kitts and Nevis in the tense and troublesome period which can be traced from December 6, 2012 to February 18, 2015.This latest crisis had its antecedents in the endemic political tribalism that is a feature of the politics of the twin-island state and which in turn can be traced back to 1882 when the British government lumped the islands of St Kitts, Nevis and Anguilla together in an act of administrative convenience. How each of these islands sought over the period to disentangle itself from these arrangements and the political alliances their leaders forged to achieve this end, is part of the attempt to answer the question "How did we get here?".

In analyzing the detrimental effects of this political tribalism, the weaknesses in our existing constitution which effectively creates an 'elective dictatorship' are identified as a contributing factor, saved only by the critical role played by the Courts as the only truly independent branch of government.

Part Two looks forward to the future and identifies some of the weaknesses in our systems and why these need to be addressed if St Kitts and Nevis is to break the cycle of patronage and tribalism and avoid similar political crises as the one that characterized the 26-month election. Here the focus is on practical recommendations for constitutional and electoral reform and improvements in the governance systems to create greater accountability and transparency. This can only be achieved with the full involvement of civil society if the country is to reverse the tribal trends and to promote issue-based politics. The effects of the country's dysfunctional political system on social and economic development are discussed, as is the weakness of the country's social contract that has contributed to the rise in violent crime. In the end, there is cautious optimism that the new government comprising an alliance of three disparate political parties will bring about some, if not all the fundamental changes needed to create a true democracy for St Kitts and Nevis and reduce the likelihood of future political crises.

Charles Wilkin QC
Basseterre, June 2015

Acknowledgements

I am deeply grateful to my wife Shermine who gave me space and tolerated my sometimes surly mood as I wrote, and for the encouragement of my mother, Aggie Kelsick, who at 93 remains a model of unremitting love. I am deeply indebted to the outstanding lawyers in my firm: Emile Ferdinand QC, Elizabeth Kelsick, Damian Kelsick, Keisha Spence and my son Garth, with whom I discussed many of the legal issues involved and whose counsel has been invaluable. I also express gratitude to my close friends who encouraged and debated the issues with me, including Felix Redmill and my legal colleague Don Mitchell QC from whose literary experience I benefitted.

I thank attorney-at-law Talibah Byron for providing me with information on the litigation referred to in the chronology and my assistants Sophia Bass and Kishma Richardson who provided their computer skills. Thanks also to my daughter Chazzette for her help with the photgraphs.

Charles and Shermine Wilkin

Dedication

This book is dedicated to the memory of my late father, Calvin Wilkin, MBE, who inspired me by his humble manner and his deep commitment to St. Kitts and Nevis. It is also dedicated to the memory of the late James Campbell, my law tutor at Pembroke College, Cambridge and to my late stepfather and mentor, Frederick Kelsick QC, both of whom taught me to think independently and to express myself fearlessly.

List of Acronyms

CARICOM	Caribbean Community
CBC	Constituency Boundaries Commission
CBI	Citizenship By Investment
CCJ	Caribbean Court of Justice
CCM	Concerned Citizens Movement
CFB	Clarence Fitzroy Bryant
CIC	Chamber of Industry and Commerce
CSME	Caribbean Single Market and Economy
IAAF	International Amateur Athletics Federation
MONC	Motion of No Confidence
NCC	National Competitiveness Council
NHC	National Housing Corporation
NIA	Nevis Island Assembly
NRP	Nevis Reformation Party
OECS	Organization of Eastern Caribbean States
PAM	People's Action Movement
PLP	People's Labour Party
SIDF	Sugar Industry Diversification Foundation
SKELEC	St. Kitts Electricity Company Limited
UDI	Unilateral Declaration of Independence
WIBC	West Indies Cricket Board

PART ONE

The 26 Month Election and the Antecedents of Political Tribalism in St Kitts and Nevis

Team Unity celebrating victory

1. Events of the 26 Month Election

St. Kitts and Nevis has a unicameral legislature known as the National Assembly. It is made up of elected members known as 'Representatives' and nominated members known as 'Senators'. In December 2012 , the Assembly was made up of eleven Representatives and three Senators two of whom were nominated by the governing party and one by the Opposition. Under the constitution, Senators can vote on all matters before the Assembly except a 'Motion of No Confidence' (MONC). An MONC can be brought at any time to challenge the support of the government in the Assembly. If a majority of Representatives vote in favour of the MONC the Prime Minister must, within three days, either resign or advise the Governor General to dissolve the Assembly. Dissolution of the Assembly triggers a General Election which must be called within 90 days.

What is hereafter described as The 26 Month Election began in December 2012 when the Opposition in the Assembly filed an MONC in the government of Prime Minister Dr Denzil Douglas whose Labour Party and its allied Nevis Reformation Party then held seven of the eleven elected seats in the National Assembly. The last General Election having been held in January 2010 and the Assembly so elected first met in March 2010, it meant that the ruling party's term could last until early June 2015 unless cut short by a successful MONC or by dissolution of the Assembly at the Prime Minister's request, if he decided to hold an earlier election.

Despite having a nominal majority in the Assembly, all was not well within Douglas' Labour Party. It was well known that Douglas had fallen out with the Deputy Prime Minister Sam Condor and the senior Minister Timothy Harris. Matters came to a head in September 2012 when Douglas introduced in the Assembly 'land for debt' legislation whereby 1200 acres of government owned land would be transferred to the National Bank in the discharge of a portion of the public debt.

Both Harris and Condor opposed the legislation and neither was present in the Assembly when the Bill was passed late in the night of September 21, 2012. Four months later, Douglas fired Harris from the Cabinet. Condor resigned shortly after. Both then formed their own political party, the People's Labour Party (PLP). Harris and Condor and the four other opposition Representatives publicly declared their intention to vote for the MONC and with six of the eleven elected members supporting the motion, Douglas faced certain defeat. Determined not to lose control of the government by way of a 'no confidence' motion Douglas delayed debate on the motion for as long as he could. He delayed for 26 months.

The constitution does not stipulate a time within which a MONC must be debated and voted on in the Assembly. It is however, a convention of the Westminster system, on which the St. Kitts and Nevis system is patterned, that an MONC should be speedily debated and voted – a practice that need not be spelled out in the constitution. Douglas and his supporters were obviously aware of this convention but chose to ignore it. The Speaker, Curtis Martin displayed his loyalty to Douglas and his lack of respect for the convention by refusing to place the MONC on the order paper for debate in the Assembly. There were peaceful demonstrations against the delay; civil society groups protested by writing to the Commonwealth Secretariat and other international bodies. The Opposition protested to the Caribbean Community (Caricom) but that club of Prime Ministers who make up that body said nothing publicly and continued to welcome Douglas into its fold. The Commonwealth Secretary-General visited St. Kitts and appeared on camera with Douglas giving the impression that the Secretariat did not care. In the absence of regional and international pressure, Douglas became even more emboldened. He was by then, the longest serving Prime Minister in the Caribbean and the Commonwealth having been first appointed to that office in 1995.

The Opposition took the matter and the Government to the High Court. The Speaker defended the litigation on the grounds that the Court could not tell him when to bring the MONC to the Assembly. At the same time however, clearly to achieve further delay, he argued that he was interested in hearing what the Court had to say and had decided therefore, that until the Court ruled, he would not table the MONC. It was a novel and flatulent application of the *sub judice* rule. The Opposition then sought to withdraw the case but despite their argument that the Court had no authority to order the Speaker to table the MONC and despite telling the public that the case was holding up the tabling of the MONC, the government and the Speaker argued that the case should continue and so it did.

In dragging out the litigation, Douglas was playing for time. His aim was to change the electoral boundaries to enhance the chances of his party in the next election. The boundaries had not been changed for over 20 years although the constitution establishes a Boundaries Commission whose duty it was to review the boundaries and to submit a report at intervals of not less than two nor more than five years. Douglas had sought to change the boundaries shortly before the 2010 General Election – a move that was struck down by the Court.

In order to continue the business of the Assembly (except the MONC) and to counter the loss of Condor and Harris, Douglas sought to increase the number of Senators in the Assembly by introducing legislation to increase the number of government senators from two to four with two for the Opposition. That would allow him to pass legislation and the annual budget and to change the boundaries while he delayed the MONC. The result was two years of litigation over the MONC, the increase of Senators, and the boundary changes. The litigation was brought by individual members of the three opposition parties: the People's Action Movement (PAM), the People's Labour Party (PLP) and the Concerned Citizen's Movement(CCM). The three parties agreed to work together under the name 'Team Unity' and selected Timothy Harris as its leader. A full chronology of that litigation is given at the end of this chapter.

Fast forward to the beginning of 2015, by which time Douglas had lost the litigation over the Senators Bill but had used another means of getting a third Senator in the person of the Attorney General Jason Hamilton. With the resulting majority of eight to seven in the combined number of Representatives and Senators he had managed to keep his overall majority in the Assembly while ignoring the MONC and dragging out the litigation over it.

Douglas had failed in his most recent attempt to change the boundaries. With his term in its final half year, he was still bent on trying yet again to change the boundaries through his control by a three to two majority on the Boundaries Commission. Boundary changes can be brought into effect by a report of the Boundaries Commission approved by the National

Assembly followed by signature of the Governor General and publication in the official Gazette. When brought into effect in that manner the new boundaries take effect on the next dissolution of the Assembly. Getting the report of the Boundaries Commission and the approval of the Assembly and the signature of the Governor General was no problem for Douglas. What concerned him was the possibility that the Opposition would, as had happened in 2009 and 2014, go to Court and get an injunction to restrain the changes until their case challenging same could be heard.

Douglas interpreted Section 50(7) of the constitution to mean that the validity of the proclamation of the new boundaries he was intending to impose could not be challenged in court after it had been signed by the Governor General and published in the official Gazette. He conjured a plan which he thought would take advantage of that section and shut out the Courts. The Boundaries Commission held a meeting at short notice on January 16, 2015 and quickly passed a report of boundary changes by a vote of three to two. The Speaker was lined up to call an emergency meeting of the Assembly the same afternoon to approve the report for which notice was given to some Representatives on the Opposition side at the last moment and to others after the Assembly meeting had actually begun. Some Opposition members made it to the sitting and protested the indecent haste with which the government was proceeding. The Speaker silenced the Opposition and put the report to the vote which was approved and signed immediately after by the Governor General. At the same time the Governor General, on Douglas' request dissolved the Assembly. Douglas gleefully announced on the steps of Government Headquarters that the report was law and the Assembly was dissolved enabling him, in his mind, to prevent the Court from intervening.

The Opposition filed an application for an interim injunction which was granted by the High Court to restrain the proclamation by the Governor General of the boundary changes. Madame Justice Carter ordered both sides to appear before the Court on January 22 for further consideration of the matter. On that date the judge heard legal arguments but reserved her decision until January 27 at which time she discharged the injunction. This meant that Douglas could proceed with the election under the new boundaries. He proceeded on the same day to announce February 16, 2015 as the date for the election. Nomination Day was declared as February 6.

The Opposition took the matter to the Court of Appeal. In a decision on February 5, that Court refused to intervene but ordered that two lists be prepared, one on the old boundaries, and the other on the new ones in order to facilitate the outcome either way of an appeal by the Opposition to the Privy Council in London, the country's final court. The Privy Council heard the appeal on February 11, broadcast live via the internet and seen by thousands of nationals.On the following day the Privy Council handed down its judgement reinstating the injunction, meaning that the General Election had to be held on the old boundaries. The Law Lords decided that the boundaries report approved by the Assembly and signed by the Governor General with the boundary changes had not been properly published in the official Gazette until January 20. The new boundaries had therefore not taken effect on January 16, as contended by the government. When they were published on January 20, the Assembly was already dissolved. They could not therefore govern the General Election of February 16.

Douglas had not been obliged by law to dissolve the Assembly on January 16, 2015. He could have waited another four months but he had confidently played that card on January 16th. His plan had failed and he had now to proceed with the election on the old boundaries.

Having failed to change the boundaries, Douglas then had to rely on his traditional party support buttressed by his huge election war chest of money which he had been augmenting over the prior two years while he avoided the MONC. The war chest also enabled him to fly in overseas voters, that is, citizens living abroad but allowed by the law to register to vote. Over 20 chartered aircraft flew in overseas voters (estimated at ten per cent of the electorate) whom Douglas expected would turn the tide in his favour. During the election campaign huge sums of money and gifts were doled out widely among resident voters. All of this was to no avail as the 'Team Unity' comprising three opposition parties led by Timothy Harris, won seven of the eleven elected seats, handing Douglas his first defeat in twenty years.

The election itself was not without drama. Wingrove George, Douglas' hand-picked Supervisor of Elections, left to his own devices by the Electoral Commission, delayed the vote count on election night. When it became apparent from the counts at the various constituency centres that the governing party was losing, George ceased to announce the results and left his post. The government TV station ceased transmission for the night but this did not prevent opponents of the Labour Party from finding other broadcast media to announce the results.

By daybreak, the country knew that Douglas had lost the election but there was enormous tension and widespread fears that another plan was being hatched to keep the ruling party in power. The Caribbean leaders finally broke their silence; Roosevelt Skerrit of Dominica, Keith Mitchell of Grenada, Ralph Gonsalves of St Vincent and the Grenadines and Kamla Persad Bissessar of Trinidad and Tobago spoke publicly that day calling on Douglas to respect the result of the election. The delinquent Supervisor did not formally announce the result on radio until late in the afternoon of February 17 and even then he announced only the winners of each constituency and not the numbers of votes. Douglas made a concession speech shortly after. The Supervisor delayed further and did not present his formal report to the Governor General until February 18 after which on that same day Timothy Harris was sworn in as the new Prime Minister. The new Cabinet was sworn in on February 21. The election saga was brought to an end on March 5 when the numbers of votes in each constituency were finally published.

The new Assembly met for the first time on May 14, 2015. Douglas, now Leader of the Opposition, boycotted the sitting at which a new Speaker Franklin Brand was elected. The new government, having requested the Queen to withdraw the appointment of Sir Edmund Lawrence as Governor General, the throne Speech was read by the Deputy Governor General Tapley Seaton.

The immediate crisis had ended but the country's underlying problems of tribal politics, a porous electoral system, a weak governance system, a widespread entitlement mentality, declining social discipline and low productivity remained. This latest political crisis was the third since Statehood in 1967 and for only the third time since then, the country has elected a new government. Like the previous two governments at the beginning of their tenure, this current government has promised to address these endemic problems but this time, the government has gone further and has promised to make the most meaningful change possible, that is to limit the Prime Minister to two terms in office. Previous governments quickly fell into the entrenched partisan ways with the leaders consolidating power around themselves and their close associates. Will the new Prime Minister, Timothy Harris and his Team Unity government do the same? The jury is out and the clock is ticking.

Prime Minister Dr.Denzil Douglas 1995, Courtesy of The National Archives, St.Kitts

CHRONOLOGY OF EVENTS OF THE 26 MONTH ELECTION

December 6, 2012	Opposition files Motion of No Confidence (MONC).
December 10, 2012	Speaker says by letter to Leader of Opposition that parliamentary rules not followed. He recognises that such a Motion should be entertained at the earliest convenient time.
December 11, 2012	Opposition re-files MONC.
December 19, 2012	Prime Minister Douglas addresses luncheon meeting of St. Kitts-Nevis Chamber of Industry & Commerce and acknowledges that MONC should be debated in the National Assembly expeditiously.
January 12, 2013	*Observer* newspaper reports that Senators (Increase of Number) Bill on Order paper as lone business of a sitting of the Assembly scheduled for January 15, 2013. The Bill seeks to add three Senators, two appointed by the Government and one by Opposition. The Bill had been given first reading on November 21, 2012. Douglas was reported as saying that new senators needed to shore up the administrative management of the Assembly and to facilitate election of a Deputy Speaker. By then it was public knowledge that the real reason was that he could not rely on support of Sam Condor and Timothy Harris and wanted two votes in the Assembly to make up the possible loss of their votes.
January 26, 2013	Douglas fires Timothy Harris from Cabinet.
January 28, 2013	Jason Hamilton sworn in as Senator and Attorney General with the intent of giving the Government side an additional vote in the Assembly. That vote would be needed to pass the Senators Bill if Condor and Harris voted against it.

January 29, 2013	Senators Bill passed by Assembly with Hamilton voting, giving the Government side an eight to seven majority. Condor and Harris voted against the Bill.
January 31, 2013	Condor resigns his ministerial positions. Condor brings a constitutional motion challenging the validity of the Senators Act.
January 31, 2013	St Kitts & Nevis Chamber of Industry & Commerce (CIC) writes to Douglas demanding that MONC be tabled for debate without further delay.
February 1, 2013	Sam Condor and Shawn Richards (Leader of the Opposition PAM Party) file an application to the High Court for an ex parte injunction to stop the Government from taking any action pursuant to the Senators Act.
February 3, 2013	St. Kitts Christian Council and St. Kitts Evangelical Association jointly write to Prime Minister Douglas demanding that MONC be tabled for debate without further delay.
February 4, 2013	Douglas replies to the CIC. Calls CIC "*a group of emotionally charged activists*". Says that he wishes to have the MONC considered but Budget must be next on the Parliamentary schedule. Douglas says that Government exists as a result of the will of the people.
February 4, 2013	Condor and Richards file a claim in the High Court for orders relating to the Senators Act including an order declaring it unconstitutional and invalid and nullifying appointments made under it.
February 11, 2013	St. Kitts & Nevis Bar Association writes to Speaker and Douglas demanding that MONC be tabled without further delay.
February 28, 2013	High Court rules that Senators Act unconstitutional and strikes it down. Court also nullifies the appointment of Hamilton as a Senator and as

Attorney General. Carty, a Government nominee, resigns as Senator and Hamilton appointed in his place. Hamilton then made Attorney General opening up another seat as Senator available to Government. Carty re-appointed Senator to fill the vacant seat restoring the eight to seven support for the Government on all matters except the MONC on which only elected members can vote.

March 1, 2013   Six of the eleven elected members of the Assembly write to Governor General indicating that they support MONC and will vote in favour of it when brought before the Assembly.

March 7, 2013   CIC, St. Kitts Christian Council, St. Kitts Evangelical Association and St. Kitts & Nevis Hotel & Tourism Association write to Secretary General of the Commonwealth and Heads of other regional and international organisations notifying them of the situation in St. Kitts & Nevis resulting from the filing of the MONC and the delay in tabling same. Letter says that further delay will in their opinion threaten the rule of law and undermine democracy in St. Kitts & Nevis. This reflects widely held opinion within the St. Kitts & Nevis communities.

April 3, 2013   Six Opposition members of the Assembly file a claim in the High Court asking the Court for relief including a declaration that the MONC must be scheduled for debate in the Assembly as a matter of urgency (the *"MONC Claim"*).

April 9, 2013   Budget session held in the Assembly.

April 15, 2013   Speaker and Government file an application in the High Court to strike out the MONC Claim.

June 11, 2013   Opposition Assembly members who brought MONC claim write to Speaker raising their grave concern at the failure to table the MONC.

June 24, 2013   Speaker writes to Leader of the Opposition saying that since the Opposition Members had brought the MONC Claim the matter of the MONC was before the Court and any debate on the MONC would have to await the Court's decision.

July 4, 2013   Opposition Assembly members file a Notice of Discontinuance of their MONC Claim.

July 8, 2013   Speaker makes a Statement in the Assembly saying that the High Court has no jurisdiction to hear any matter concerning the exercise of the Speaker's discretion and cannot compel him to table the MONC, but the Opposition should not have discontinued the MONC Claim and he wants to hear what the Court has to say on the exercise of his powers. In the meantime he will not table the MONC nor permit any debate on any matter relating to the MONC.

July 9, 2013   Despite Speaker's statement that Court cannot tell him what to do with the MONC, Attorney General files applications to the High Court for an Order to set aside the Notice of Discontinuance and to proceed with hearing of his application to strike out the MONC Claim. He says that it is the public interest that the Court hears his application rather than allowing the MONC Claim to be discontinued.

September 5, 2013   Report of Constituency Boundaries Commission (CBC) on the change of constituency boundaries approved by a majority of the five members of the CBC.

September 9, 2013   Injunction obtained by Opposition Assembly members to prevent Governor General from making a proclamation of the CBC report.

September 11, 2013 Opposition moves the High Court for leave to apply for judicial review to quash the report of the CBC (the *"Boundaries case"*).

November 25, 2013	Opposition granted leave to apply for judicial review.
December 16, 2013	Court hears Attorney General's application on the MONC Claim.
February 12, 2014	Court rules that the MONC Claim should not be wholly discontinued but should continue against the Speaker only. The Court declares the law to be that the Court does have power to hear the matter and to determine if the constitutional rights of the Opposition members have been infringed. The Court finds as a matter of law that each and every member of the Assembly is entitled by the constitution to request that a MONC be placed before the Assembly and that such a Motion must be accorded priority over other business by being scheduled, debated and voted on within a reasonable time given the programme of the Assembly. The Court says that while its ruling did not conclude the case it expected that the Speaker would accept the ruling and act accordingly in tabling the MONC.
February 26, 2014	Attorney General applies for leave to appeal against the MONC decision and to stay proceedings in the MONC Claim pending hearing of the appeal. Speaker does same next day.
March 20, 2014	Leave to appeal granted by Court of Appeal to Attorney General and Speaker (no objection by Opposition Assembly members).
May 15, 2014	Court hears Boundaries case.
July 3, 2014	Court of Appeal grants stay of proceedings in MONC Claim.
July 31, 2014	Court declares the Boundaries report of the CBC null and void and quashes it. The Court also finds that the Opposition has failed to show an appearance of bias on the part of the CBC

Chairman, Peter Jenkins.

September 5, 2014	Opposition members who brought the Boundaries case file an appeal to the Court of Appeal against the decision of the High Court that CBC Chairman Peter Jenkins not biased.
September 23, 2014	Attorney General and the CBC file an appeal to the Court of Appeal against the decision of the High Court quashing the CBC Boundaries Report.
October 27, 2014	Court of Appeal hears MONC Claim appeals by Speaker and Attorney General, dismisses them and orders MONC Claim to proceed to trial.
October 30, 2014	Court of Appeal hears appeal by Government from judgment of High Court quashing Senators Act. Judgment reserved. Judgment not delivered as at February 16, 2015 but later the Court of Appeal upholds the decision of the Judge that the Senators Act was unconstitutional.
November 17, 2014	Attorney General applies to be re-instated as a party in the MONC Claim.
November 26, 2014	Leave granted to Attorney General. Trial of MONC Claim set for January 19–20, 2015.
January 16, 2015	Constituency Boundaries Commission meets and submits report at 3.45 pm. Majority of CBC (three of five) support boundary changes.

Emergency and abbreviated meeting of Assembly convened in haste without proper notice to all Opposition Assembly members and without proper debate. New boundaries approved over protest by Opposition members that their rights trampled on. Some Opposition members not allowed to address the Assembly.

CBC's boundaries report immediately promulgated by Governor General (GG) and Government says it has been gazetted to bring it into law at 6.30pm.

GG simultaneously dissolves Assembly

At 7.40 pm, after time Government says Gazette published, High Court Judge Carter grants temporary injunction on application of Opposition. Return date set for January 22, 2015 for parties to appear before Judge.

January 19, 2015	Trial date for MONC Claim. Speaker and AG argue that Assembly was dissolved on January 16, 2015 with result that MONC no longer in effect and MONC Claim therefore moot. Opposition Assembly members oppose that argument. Court rules case to continue with trial at a future date to be set. Claim had not been tried by February 16, 2015.
January 22, 2015	Justice Carter hears application by Government to lift boundaries injunction. Reserves decision to January 27, 2015.
January 27, 2015	Justice Carter lifts injunction. Refuses to replace it pending appeal. GG immediately issues writs of election. Election date of February 16, 2015 announced. Nomination day to be February 6, 2015.
January 28, 2015	Opposition appeals to Court of Appeal against ruling of Justice Carter.
January 29, 2015	Court of Appeal grants interlocutory injunction to suspend proclamation of new boundaries and sets February 9, 2015 as date of hearing of appeal.
January 30, 2015	Douglas announces that Government asking for Court of Appeal to bring forward date of hearing of appeal.
February 2, 2015	Court of Appeal advances hearing to February 4, 2015.
February 4, 2015	Court of Appeal hears appeal
February 5, 2015	Court of Appeal discharges its temporary injunction

and allows proclamation of new boundaries to stand. Grants leave to Opposition to appeal to Privy Council. Pending the appeal to the Privy Council Court of Appeal orders nominations to proceed on February 6, 2015 on basis of new list (with boundary changes) but Supervisor to have a second list prepared on the basis of the old boundaries and to hold it pending ruling of Privy Council.

February 11, 2015   Privy Council hears appeal in London.

February 12, 2015   Privy Council rules. Stays proclamation of new boundaries and restores the injunction imposed by the High Court. Election therefore to be held on old boundaries.

February 16, 2015   Election held peacefully. Without explanation from Supervisor of Elections to waiting electorate, counts delayed. First results not announced until just before 11pm. Results trickle in over the next few hours causing great concern as to why it should take so long to count 30,000 votes.

February 17, 2015   At approximately 3.30am, with only three of the eleven seats officially declared, but with reports from the counts showing that the opposition Team Unity likely to win the election, Supervisor of Elections says (via Government owned ZIZ TV) that no further results will be announced until further notice. He leaves his post. Quite naturally this creates severe tension in the country with many fearing sabotage of the election and unrest. Later in the morning civil society organizations write expressing disgust at this abdication of duty and demanding that Supervisor announce the results. They call on Electoral Commission to direct him to do so. Prime Ministers Gonsalves of St. Vincent and the Grenadines, Mitchell of Grenada and Skerrit of Dominica and (later in the day) Prime Minister Persad Bissessar of Trinidad and Tobago make public broadcasts from their respective countries calling on Supervisor to announce the results and on Douglas to respect the verdict of the people. Nothing was heard publicly from Douglas in the morning (not even to tell the Supervisor to act properly) but, to his credit, Nigel Carty, the Deputy Chairman of the Labour Party, came on air in mid morning and conceded the election. Nothing further heard from Supervisor nor the Electoral Commission until 4.45pm when Supervisor announces results showing Team Unity candidates winning seven of the eleven seats with Labour/NRP winning four. Supervisor withholds the actual numbers of votes for each candidate. Shortly after, Douglas broadcast a concession speech. Supervisor says he has until the end of February 18, 2015 to report results to Governor General. Country still severely tense.

February 18, 2015   Prime Minister Harris sworn in at Government House at 5pm. Country begins to exhale.

March 5, 2015   Full results published by Supervisor.

April 17, 2015   Court of Appeal delivers judgment and upholds the decision of the High Court to quash the Senators Act.

May 11, 2015   Privy Council delivers the reasons for its decision of February 12, 2015. Finds that the boundaries report was legally proclaimed only on January 20, 2015 when the Official Gazette containing it became available to the public at the office of the Government Information Service. At that time the National Assembly had already been dissolved. The boundaries report could not therefore apply to the General Election of February 16, 2015. The Privy Council rejected the argument of the Government that section 50(7) of the Constitution ousted the jurisdiction of the Court to hear any challenge to the boundaries report. The Privy Council held that section 18 of the Constitution gives the Court jurisdiction to protect fundamental rights and that power is unaffected by section 50(7). The boundaries report can also be subject to judicial review.

Swearing-in of Prime Minister Harris

Team Unity Rally for MONC

Team Unity: (L-R) Michael Perkins, Wendy Phipps, Shawn Richards, Mark Brantley, Timothy Harris, Eugene Hamilton, Lindsay Grant, Ian Liburd, Vincent Byron Jr., Vance Amory.

The Tribal Politics of St. Kitts and Nevis

S t. Kitts and Nevis are among the most charming and beautiful parts of the earth. The islands have a pleasant and healthy climate. The lifestyle is easygoing and the people are warm and friendly, except when it comes to politics.

The 26 Month Election showed graphically that political tribalism is still very much part of the culture in St. Kitts and Nevis, as evidenced by the vicious nature of the election campaign and by the ruthless machinations of the electoral process. The atrocious and disgusting misbehaviour of the Supervisor of Elections (who should never hold any public office again) and of those who conspired with him or allowed him to frustrate the announcement of results and the swearing in of the new government, is further evidence of the potentially destructive effect of the tribalism which has continued in the behaviour of some diehards on both sides since the election.

Except for a century and a half when the British shared St. Kitts with the French, the islands were British colonies for close to 350 years up to 1967. Then under international pressure and with their declining economic value, Britain granted the islands Associated Statehood in conjunction with Anguilla. Associated Statehood gave the state of St. Kitts-Nevis-Anguilla full internal self-government with Britain retaining responsibility only for defence and external affairs. Full independence followed in 1983.

The British laid the groundwork for turmoil by failing in the arrangements for Associated Statehood to address effectively the concerns of Anguilla which had been lumped with St. Kitts and Nevis in 1882, purely for administrative convenience. Neither Anguilla nor Nevis wanted such an association and both islands protested with justification that after the introduction of universal adult suffrage in 1952, they were neglected by the central government in St. Kitts led by the Labour Party which never won a seat on either island. Thus,

Associated Statehood began in turmoil which was the initial source of the political irrationality from which the country still suffers

The association of Anguilla with St. Kitts and Nevis was ended in the period between statehood and independence. That period was also marked by growing political controversy between St. Kitts and Nevis. As fate would have it, Nevis held the balance of power at the time of independence and was able to influence, in the independence constitution, an unbalanced "Federation" weighted in its favour. As a result, while the British have been gone nearly 50 years, the country, disquietened by a turbulent birth and manipulated by leaders bent on continuing the political polarization, has remained unsettled.

Human nature is the biggest obstacle to democracy but this fact is so often overlooked. The attraction of and craving for power often overwhelm the qualities of humility and respect for power which are more consistent with democracy. Excessive egos can overwhelm even the most educated of individuals and many leaders have gained power with the most noble of ideals but, once it has been achieved, become carried away by it. The passion and negative behaviour which election campaigns generate can make individuals callous and indifferent to criticism. King Short Shirt, the great Antiguan calypsonian in *Power and Authority*, one of his most outstanding calypsos, put it this way:

> Power rules the world today
> Power corrupts they say
> And absolute power corrupts you absolutely
> It can change a man who has a heart of gold
> Make him cruel, wicked, self centered and cold.

Most human beings are by nature followers rather than questioners. Often large numbers of people are so captivated by the influence of a leader or a political party or by allegiance to a group, be it because of family tradition or for ethnic, social or ideological reasons, that they fail to question the plans and ideas presented by the party they support or to listen to the opposing views. Hence attitudes can limit the effectiveness of a democracy and where the prevailing attitudes of a country permit, its democracy can be usurped by ruthless or power hungry individuals. Franklin Roosevelt thought that the real safeguard of democracy is education, but history has shown that view to be simplistic. Education does not necessarily overcome the tribe mentality nor, it seems from the early evidence of the Information Age, does the ready access to information provided by modern technology. St. Kitts and Nevis boasts a literacy rate of 98 per cent and universal, free secondary education but you would not believe that based on the politics alone.

Even allowing for the relatively short period of its self-rule and for the complexities of democracy, St. Kitts and Nevis has thus far failed to achieve real maturity in its constitutional democracy. This is in large measure due to the deep and bitter political tribalism that by all standards, regional and international, is unhealthy and damaging. That tribalism has exposed and aggravated the basic weaknesses in the constitution. It has demonstrated all the vulnerabilities of democracy and the flaws of human nature referred to above.

The extent of the polarization was graphically described by Anglican priest Father Alrick Francis in an interview on *Winn Fm* radio station on February 13, 2014. Referring to life in Nevis, Father Francis told the reporter that in the previous seven years or so, Nevis had changed from a close knit to a divided society. He said there were tensions all over the island and people were boiling and angry and losing their sense of relationship. People even refused to greet each other in church and selected their churches and denominations based on politics. According to Father Francis, they even choose seats in church based on their political allegiance. What he described then, is a phenomenon that has existed in St. Kitts for almost half a century having taken root in the very year of Associated Statehood following the events of June 10,1967. The fact that it has proved contagious and spread to Nevis should not surprise anyone given the proximity and the size of the two islands and the governance system they share. That it took so long is probably due to the difference in outlook of the people of St. Kitts and of Nevis and the differences in their history over the past century.

The prevailing culture has managed not only to put party above all else but to mix God into the politics. Political leaders can do no wrong and must not admit error. One was even portrayed as providing blessings. Love, forgiveness and humility, which are at the core of Christianity, have no place in political activity. God is regarded by each side as being on its side.

The story of the Basseterre High School is an example of how politics transcends even health. The school was closed twice in 2012 and 2014 because it posed a health hazard to students and teachers. However, before the first closure and between the first and second episodes, persons complaining that the school was contaminated were accused of playing politics , its teachers accused of being psychosomatic and a prominent dermatologist who had run for public office was accused of putting her politics above her medical oath. One would have thought that the authorities would from the outset, err on the side of caution. Instead they bunkered down politically at first but then relented and closed the school. It took two years and unquantified grief and outside intervention for good sense to prevail. The school remains closed as at June 2015.

Even death cannot avoid the scourge of this political tribalism. There have been coffins dressed in party political colours and mourners forsaking the usual dark colours for party colours. I was reliably told of a conversation in Charlestown, the capital of Nevis, between a social activist and a gang member in the height of a period of gang terror. A funeral procession passed during the conversation. The gang member said pointing to the mourners dressed in party colors "What about that gang?". *Touché*.

It is said, and I agree, that a country is only as strong as its civil society. Civil society should by its influence contribute to the checks and balances on the executive. Its organs should promote good governance and the responsible exercise of democratic freedoms and fundamental rights. The civil society of St. Kitts and Nevis has been relatively ineffectual because the political tribalism has embedded itself within the constituent bodies and many who are unaffected by tribalism remain quiet out of fear. Many of the politicians appear to give deference to civil society but, below the surface, seek to undermine its constituent organisations. For example, some members of the Bar Association refuse to participate in its activities because they hold the view that the Bar has no business commenting on issues in a political dispute, even if they relate to the constitution and the law. This occurs despite one of the express purposes given to the association in its empowering statute being *'to promote, maintain and support the administration of justice and the rule of law'*. If lawyers are so narrow-minded and cowed one should not be surprised that many others in civil society are no different. The doctors are not organized and do not speak with one voice even on health issues and business organisations such as the Chamber of Industry and Commerce and the Hotel and Tourism

Association have not been as impactful as they should be on matters of national importance. In summary, civil society has not contributed as it should to the promotion of democracy.

The media should be a positive influence for good in a democracy. The St. Kitts and Nevis media is a relatively young one and it is only in the past 20 years that media organisations independent of the government have sprung up. Before that the only real media were the government owned radio and TV stations that were then and still are, purely government mouthpieces, despite the constitutional requirement that they be available to the political Opposition and to the people. Here again *'the people'* is in practice, limited to select people. The appendix to this book contains the famous 'Four Seasons Accord' by which the violent political uprising in St. Kitts, following general elections in 1993, was meant to be settled. It called for the government media to be de-politicized. It should not surprise the reader that the only aspect of that agreement that was implemented was that a general election be held within 18 months.

In the face of the government spin machine and in the absence of freedom of information legislation, the media ought to play a key role in ferreting out the truth, protecting the fundamental right of free speech and enhancing democracy. However with a few notable exceptions (the radio station *Winn Fm* being one) the standard of journalism is substantially below international standards and hence the impact of the growing media has not been as strong as it should be. The expansion of social media has widened communication but has hardly improved the level of dialogue.

The sprinter, Kim Collins is the face of St. Kitts and Nevis to the world. However grandiose the politicians may think they are, Kim is indisputably the best known Kittitian on earth. His victory in the 100 metres final in the IAAF World Athletics Championships in 2003 amazed the world. His continued success in athletics for well over a decade has brought enormous credit and recognition to the country. Yet even he was dragged into the tribal politics and painted as an Opposition supporter when in 2008 the government refused to name the newly built national athletics stadium after him, giving it the spurious name of Silver Jubilee. His name was put on a stand in the stadium as a token. Following the 26 Month Election this grave error was corrected and the stadium was renamed in honour of Kim.

Sir Fred Phillips, was the first Governor of the Associated State of St. Kitts-Nevis-Anguilla. After he demitted that office, Sir Fred became an outstanding constitutional lawyer and regionalist who contributed to the jurisprudence of the region. He served in various other capacities in the private and public sectors up to his late eighties. Sir Fred was appointed by the Government of St. Kitts and Nevis to head a Constitutional Commission which reported, after wide consultation, in 1998 and a Constitutional Task Force which also consulted widely and reported in 1999 with recommendations on very substantial changes to the constitution.

The Task Force noted as follows on the political divisions within the country:

> The country is incredibly polarized. Virtually everything - a word spoken, to whom it is spoken, a phrase, a proposal – is scrutinized through a political magnifying glass for signs and signals, and thus for political and other attitudes and agendas. We are certain that the country wastes too much time and energy, which it cannot afford, on such activity"

In another section of the report the political polarization was referred to as the *'demon of political polarization.'*

Some of the recommendations for constitutional reform made by the Commission and the Task Force are referred to in this book. Meanwhile,the reports themselves are gathering dust on a shelf somewhere in Government Headquarters.

'Democracy must be something more than two wolves and a sheep voting on what to have for lunch' declared James Bovard , a civil libertarian in *1994*. The 'winner takes all' effect of elections has exacerbated the tribalism in St. Kitts and Nevis. Winner takes all means that the supporters of the governing party expect to get, in priority to everyone else, all the benefits available. Loyalty surpasses merit, hard work and enterprise as a means of individual progress which makes it all the more important to hold on to political power. This prevailing culture has harmed the productivity of its people and seriously impaired the competitiveness of the country. The appendix to this book contains the 2010 report of the Competitiveness Council which was a think tank established by the government to review and report on the competitiveness of the country. The Council was chaired by the writer and composed of persons from government, government controlled business entities, academia and the private sector. Its observations remain true at the time of writing in June 2015.

Tribal politics is not unique to St. Kitts and Nevis. Politics is in many places intense and hostile. Other Caribbean countries have entrenched political divisions but based on my discussions over the years with persons of knowledge in all our neighbouring countries, I can say with sad confidence that nowhere in the Caribbean is the politics as personal and nasty as it is here. I have attended sporting and other events in other Caribbean islands where the politicians mingle and their party allegiance is not apparent. They are first and foremost Antiguans or Trinidadians or Guyanese. In St. Kitts you know their allegiance for sure because there are few if any opposition politicians in the official areas.

It has to be crass immaturity for leaders in a micro state such as ours not to engage each other on issues of national importance save in the National Assembly. And even here the debate and most presentations are generally purely partisan, differing little from the grandstanding that is common on the political platform

We could do well to heed the warning given by former Jamaica Prime Minister P.J. Patterson to the joint sitting of the Jamaican Parliament held in November 2012 to pay tribute to him. He said:

> "We must abandon the adversarial approach of the past and replace it with a consensual form of politics to embrace the best ideas regardless of the political quarters from which these ideas originate. I underline this problem to warn of the dangers ahead.... If we fail to posture a political environment that discourages the brightest minds to participate in the political process, we are placing our democracy at risk."

The former Prime Minister added that politicians

> "have contributed to our sad state of affairs by our utterances here and on public platforms."

He continued

> "Personal friendships exist among many on both sides of the political divide, but how often do we say something good or positive about the initiatives of the opposing political party."

His last statement is clear evidence that Jamaica is not as polarized as St. Kitts and Nevis because there ain't no friends here on opposite sides of the political divide.

The recent history of the Sugar Industry Diversification Foundation (SIDF) shows the prevailing tribal attitude that party interest prevails, insanely in this instance, in the use of the nation's resources. It is better for the party in power to spend it all than to leave it for its opponents to inherit if they win the election. The Foundation was established in 2006 with the stated object of assisting in the diversification of the economy of St. Kitts out of the sugar industry which was closed in 2005 after 350 years as the main industry on the island. As permitted by the Citizenship Act, the Cabinet approved a donation of US$250,000 to the SIDF (inclusive of government fees) as an approved investment to qualify the donor for economic citizenship of the country under its Citizenship by Investment programme (CBI).

The government of the day portrayed SIDF as a 'private' foundation but it was and is legally and in every other respect a public fund. The portrayal of the SIDF as a private foundation had three purposes. The first was to keep the monies away from the country's Treasury and budget process. Secondly, the country had in the preceding ten years built up a huge national debt which rose to 200 per cent of GDP, the third highest in the world. Forseeing that it would have to eventually deal with its creditors, the government did not want to have a huge available balance in the Treasury and so it told its creditors that it did not control the SIDF. The creditors accepted that and so did the International Monetary Fund (IMF). The creditors took a huge haircut and the IMF advanced monies to bail out the government. The government was then unrestrained in its use of the SIDF as a public and political fund.

The third reason that the SIDF was portrayed as a private fund was because the USA and Canada had not looked kindly on citizenship by investment programmes which included direct contributions to governments. Like the IMF, the USA and Canada seem to have been persuaded that the SIDF was a private foundation and did not openly object to its use as an investment vehicle in the CBI. It turns out that the SIDF may have had another role. The investigations underway will disclose the extent to which the fund was used during the 26 Month Election for the benefit of the failed re-election campaign of the Labour Party. In May 2015 the new Prime Minister reported to the country that he found on taking office that the entire 1.47 billion dollars collected in the fund to date had been totally spent or committed.

Now that the country can exhale from the crisis of the 26 Month Election it is left to be seen if the lessons will be learned. The coalition of parties which it took to unseat Douglas bodes well for an end, if gradual, to the Labour/PAM polarization. It will be a very tall but not impossible order for Team Unity to live up to its name and to bring all sections of the communities together. That will require civil society to wake up to its important role. It will require the new opposition to play a strong but reasoned role in keeping the new government in check. If that happens our politics can become issue based rather than tribal. If that does not happen the society may not be so fortunate when the next crisis occurs, which it inevitably will.

1966 Cabinet. L-R: F.T. Williams, B.F. Dias, R.L. Bradshaw, Sir Fred Phillips, C.A. Paul Southwell, J.N France and W.F. Glasford. Courtesy of The National Archives, St.Kitts

February 27, 1967 Statehood Day Parade. Courtesy of The National Archives, St. Kitts

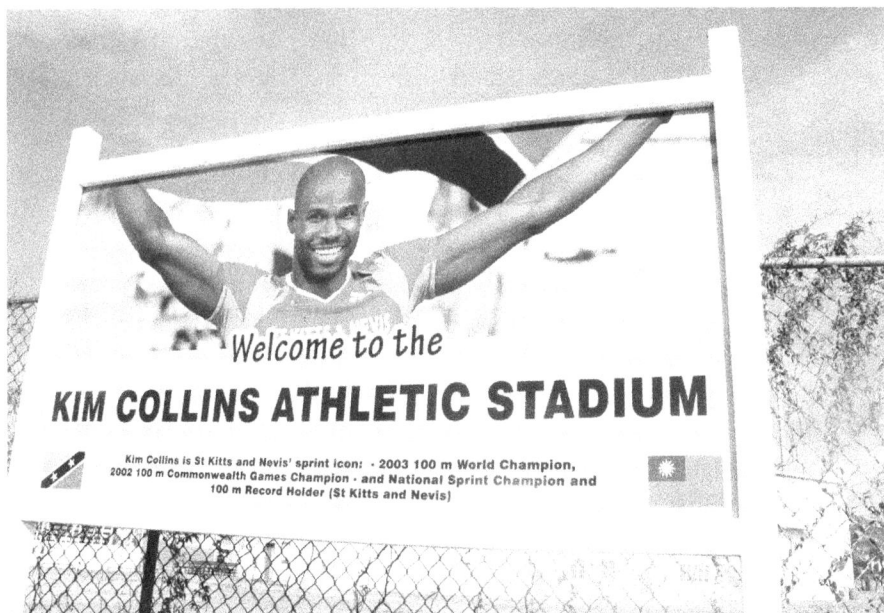

Sign for the Kim Collins Athletic Stadium

3. *The Anguilla Revolt and the Fallout from June 10, 1967*

Britain controlled the governance of up to one fifth of the people of the world during the nineteenth century and the first part of the twentieth century. After the Second World War ended in 1945 the sun set on the British Empire. Britain was virtually bankrupted by the war and the anti-colonial movement gained strength. The USA, which bailed Britain out financially after the war, and the Soviet Union, became the dominant world powers. By 1965 Britain ruled only five million people outside the UK, including the inhabitants of St. Kitts-Nevis-Anguilla which islands were colonies for more than three hundred years.

The three islands were different. St. Kitts had been a jewel in the crown because of its fertile soil and profitable sugar industry. Nevis also produced sugar but less profitably. The industry declined there leaving the lands in the control largely of the government and a peasantry. Anguilla is a coral island with rocky soil able to sustain only subsistence farming and fishing before it developed a tourism industry being blessed with some of the best beaches in the world. Despite their cash poverty the people of Anguilla owned most of their land. Together with their tough living conditions that helped to make them hardy and proud.

In the 1950s Britain developed a decolonization plan for its West Indian colonies under which the islands would be granted independence en bloc as a political federation and proceeded to establish such a union in 1958. However, the experiment was short-lived as, beset by insular politics and the clashing egos of its leaders, the withdrawal first of Jamaica and then Trinidad and Tobago shortly after, led to its collapse. The constituent members of the former federation reverted to their status as individual colonies of the UK. Barbados, the Leeward and Windward Islands flirted with a union referred to as the 'Little Eight' but that never materialized. Jamaica,

Trinidad and Tobago gained independence in 1962 while Barbados became independent in 1966. Britain then introduced the status of 'Associated Statehood' as an interim step to independence for Grenada, St. Vincent and the Grenadines, St. Lucia, Dominica, Antigua and Barbuda and St. Kitts-Nevis-Anguilla. Under this arrangement, these smaller islands were granted internal self-governance with Britain retaining responsibility for defence and external affairs.

As observed earlier, Anguilla had been part of the colony of St. Kitts-Nevis-Anguilla since 1882 but Anguillians had always resented the association with St. Kitts. Immediately prior to Associated Statehood, Anguilla had one elected representative in the legislature of the colony, St. Kitts had seven and Nevis had two. The government of the colony was dominated by the St. Kitts-Nevis Labour Party which despite its name had little support anywhere but in St. Kitts. The Labour Party was led by its charismatic and ebullient leader Robert Bradshaw who was once accused of saying that he would make Anguilla a desert and that he 'would put pepper in their soup and bones in their rice.' In fact Anguilla was, in terms of its infrastructure, not far from that; it had mainly dirt roads, no central water supply, few schools and minimal electricity. Despite its magnificent beaches there was no tourism industry and the island was effectively ignored by the Bradshaw government as was Nevis. Only the most blinkered person would deny that the Anguillians had a just cause for concern that 'Association' and then Independence as part of a state dominated by St. Kitts would result in further suffering for the people. It has been argued in defence of Bradshaw that St. Kitts had very little itself, although St. Kitts undoubtedly had much more by way of development and infrastructure than did Anguilla.

Anguillians had protested vociferously over their poor living conditions including a petition in 1958 signed by more than 3,000 Anguillians calling on the Governor of the Leeward Islands to dissolve the political association of St. Kitts with Anguilla. The petition warned that 'a people cannot live without hope for long without erupting socially' (Colville L. Petty and A. Nat Hodge, *Anguilla's Battle for Freedom 1967-1969,* Petnat, Anguilla 2010).

Anguillians were ridiculed by Kittitians who referred to them as 'Bobo Johnnies'. When I was growing up I learned derogatory jokes about Anguillians. Their accent was mocked and those who attended school with me were constantly heckled. Anguilla was regarded as a backwater community with nice beaches but Kittitians did not realise how proud, brave and independent Anguillians were. The British and St. Kitts governments mistakenly ignored that fierce pride and determination.

In September 1960, a category 4 hurricane *Donna*, devastated the island and Anguillians were very upset at what they considered the inadequate response of the central government to this disaster.

As statehood loomed, Peter Adams, the sole elected representative for Anguilla in the legislature of the Colony seemed prepared to play ball with the British and Bradshaw, but his inclination to compromise was not shared by his people. By then, a movement in Anguilla headed by the fearless Ronald Webster had begun to galvanize support for total separation from St. Kitts and for Anguilla to remain a colony of the UK. Many involved in the movement were prepared to die for the cause and to kill if necessary.

Arrangements for statehood were finalised at a constitutional conference in London in mid-1966 at which Anguilla was represented by Peter Adams. The arrangements included provisions for local councils as the principal organ of local government for Nevis and Anguilla. Those provisions were contained in section 109 of 113 sections of the statehood constitution in a chapter headed 'Miscellaneous'. One does not have to be a genius to figure out that the section was included an afterthought. Its very contents confirmed that. The membership of each Council was to be prescribed by the Legislature (controlled by St. Kitts) subject to two thirds of the membership being elected on the island it was to serve. Until January 1, 1968 each Council was to consist of such numbers as the Governor would determine and the members were to be appointed by the Governor acting in accordance with the advice of the Premier who was to consult with the Leader of the Opposition. The powers of the Council were not stated.

After the conference the Bradshaw government proposed powers for the local councils details of which were not disclosed to the Anguillian people until the end of 1966 two months prior to the commencement of Associated Statehood. There was disquiet in Anguilla that the proposed local council would be weak and ineffective and having only minor functions. They were concerned too at the lack of provision for budgetary support from the central government in St. Kitts. The British sent a representative to Anguilla a month before 'Statehood Day' (set for February 27, 1967), ostensibly to explain the proposals but he was given no real chance to do so. He was met at the airport by a large crowd of demonstrators. When later in the day he met with a group of Anguillian leaders the meeting place was stormed by an angry and hostile crowd and the meeting ended abruptly.

The Anguillians continued to take a forceful stand; a Statehood Queen Show held on February 4, 1967 was violently ended by protesters when the police had to use tear gas to disperse them. In the days following, while investigating the disruption of the event, the police were shot at, forcing the authorities to deploy additional law enforcement officers from St. Kitts and by the British. Efforts continued to resolve the situation but Statehood arrived on February 27, 1967 without any progress or a resolution.

The likelihood of trouble in Anguilla was foreseen in London but the British government was bent on getting rid of its colonies. During parliamentary debates members of the House of Commons raised the issue and expressed serious concern.Meanwhile the situation in Anguilla was creating tensions as well in St. Kitts where an opposition party called the Peoples Action Movement (PAM) had been launched and was providing the first real political opposition to Bradshaw.

On March 8, 1967 Government House in Anguilla was burned down followed by shooting incidents in the weeks following. Then on May 29, 1967 the police were expelled at gunpoint by Anguillans. According to Ronald Webster in his book *The Revolutionary Leader: Reflections on Life, Leadership and Politics* (2011, Denver, Outskirts Press), 'The Revolution had started and it was at the point of no return.' In that book Ronald Webster also said that he was a founding member of PAM. Finally on June 10, 1967 some Anguillians launched an armed attack on St. Kitts.

After these incidents,Anguilla did not return to rule by the government of the Associated State. For close to two years it was governed by a de facto government headed by Webster. A referendum was held in Anguilla on July 11, 1967, the result being 1813 votes in favour of secession and 5 against. The de facto government proclaimed a Universal Declaration of Independence (UDI) and a new constitution of an independent Anguilla. Efforts continued regionally and by direct communication between the de facto government of Anguilla and Britain to resolve the impasse. These negotiations resulted in an interim agreement which lasted through 1968 under which a British official administered the island in conjunction with the elected Council. That arrangement later ended in disagreement. As time went on it became clear that Anguilla would not return to the Associated State. A second referendum in Anguilla on February 6, 1969 produced a similar result as the earlier one, this time 1739 in favour of the UDI and 4 against. Webster declared Anguilla an independent nation. Despite the second UDI the Anguillians made it clear that their preferred position was to return to colonial status.

Losing patience, the British sent a junior cabinet minister William Whitlock to Anguilla on March 11, 1969. The Anguillians showed up in numbers at the airport to greet him but things turned sour and Whitlock and his party (accused by the Anguillians of acting arrogantly) were chased off the island. The following week the British invaded Anguilla with over 300 paratroopers and marines landing on the beaches from two warships offshore. British police followed. Not a shot was fired. The British reimposed their rule pursuant to an Act of the British Parliament which was exactly what the Anguillians wanted. The British also undertook the infrastructure improvements that the Anguillians badly needed. The British invasion is described in the well known book *Under an English Heaven.* Pictures in the newspapers in England (where I was studying at the time) showed British troops bathing naked in the beautiful turquoise sea with their guns stuck in the shining sand. Questions were asked in the British media as to why Britain had invaded a tiny Caribbean island of mainly black people but were afraid to invade Rhodesia (present day Zimbabwe) a predominantly black country whose white minority government had similarly declared UDI. The international media was scathing in its indictment. Some Caribbean governments supported while others criticized the invasion. Whitlock lost his job in the Cabinet and it was felt that the fiasco contributed to the defeat of the Harold Wilson Government in the general election in Britain in 1970.

The question then was whether Britain would return the island to St. Kitts but it never did and the separation was formalized by the Anguilla Act of 1980 passed by the British Parliament. That Act, effective December 19, 1980, formally separated Anguilla from the Associated State of St. Kitts-Nevis- Anguilla.

It may have been a complete coincidence but the legal separation took place after Bradshaw had died in 1978 and his successor as Premier and long-standing ally in the St. Kitts labour movement Paul Southwell, had died in 1979. The successor Premier Lee Moore accepted the inevitability of the legal separation and then, as fate would have it, the Labour party lost power in St. Kitts and Nevis to a coalition of PAM and the Nevis Reformation Party (NRP).

I offer some personal views on the political dynamics affecting the Anguilla situation. The Anguillian revolutionaries were completely committed to their cause, brave in their defence of it and prepared to die for it. Webster said in his book *Revolutionary Leader* that the Anguillians constantly feared an invasion from St. Kitts. In that fear they overestimated the will of the people of St. Kitts. There were not many people in St. Kitts who were prepared to die for Bradshaw's cause to regain control of Anguilla. Clever politician that he was Bradshaw knew that only too well but had to keep that option open. He expected the British to discipline the Anguillians. The British 'hemmed' and 'hawed' for two years and then invaded. It is such an irony that Anguilla revolted not to achieve independence but to re-assert its colonial status! This showed the extent of the opposition by Anguillans, to and their distrust of St. Kitts politicians.

The Commonwealth Caribbean countries had for the most part supported Bradshaw and the integrity of St. Kitts-Nevis-Anguilla but some protested the invasion. None was prepared to support Bradshaw with force.

It baffles me why the leaders of St. Kitts wanted to hold on to Anguilla. There was absolutely no moral, strategic, electoral or economic benefit to St. Kitts in so doing. The Anguillians were the only resolute party and victory for their separatist movement was inevitable. The great pity – perhaps irony, is that in achieving their goal they set St. Kitts and Nevis up to become a continually brooding and unsettled democracy.

On May 30, 1967 in response to the unrest in Anguilla a state of emergency had been declared by the Governor of St. Kitts-Nevis-Anguilla, effective throughout the entire state and on June 6 it was extended by the House of Assembly until November 30.

In the early hours of June 10, there were armed attacks on institutions of the Government of St. Kitts-Nevis-Anguilla, namely the Police Headquarters at Cayon Street in the heart of Basseterre, the capital of St. Kitts, the Defence Force headquarters at Camp Springfield on the outskirts of Basseterre and the Power Station at Kittstoddarts near Basseterre and the airport but no one was killed. The government regarded the attacks as an attempted coup d'etat. Under emergency powers of arrest promulgated by the Governor pursuant to the state of emergency, 22 officers and associates of the Peoples Action Movement (PAM), the opposition political party on St. Kitts, were detained at Her Majesty's Prison in Basseterre known locally as 1840 Cayon Street after the year in which it was built. Four Anguillians were arrested and charged with offences related to the armed attacks. Six members of PAM and one of the Anguillians were charged with conspiracy to overthrow the government. No one was convicted of any criminal offence related to the attacks.

Much else has been said about these events. I set out some extracts from *The Labour Spokesman*, the printed mouthpiece of the ruling Labour Party and *The Democrat*, the printed mouthpiece of PAM.

The Labour Spokesman said in is report:

The Truth About "Freedom Day" And Why It Flopped

Yesterday, Monday 12th June [1967], was supposed to have been "Freedom Day", a day of rejoicing for the forces of violence, evil and disorder. From information which has recently come to light, it is clear that yesterday had been set aside for celebrations after the overthrow of the Government by force on Saturday and Sunday.

Those who had agreed to take up arms against the constitutionally and democratically elected Government of the State had already prepared a new flag, a new Cabinet and a new Civil Service hierarchy for the State.

That is what "Freedom Day" was supposed to have marked - the beginning of Government by guns and explosives, the beginning of government by terror.

But our Police Force is more loyal than these criminals want to believe, and so is our Defence Force. And the Labour Government is more firm by entrenched in the masses of the people than the forces of destruction want to believe.

So "Freedom Day" passed by without incident. Nearly all business places opened as usual, though one or two extremely bitter employers sent back home their employees who turned out to work."

The Democrat reported:

Mass Arrests Follow Shooting Incidents

What is really behind all these arrests which include the leaders of the PAM, the only opposition political party, and WAM and CURE, two workers Trade Unions not connected with Government?

The only information which is available to the public is that which is repeatedly broadcast night and day by the Premier, who alleges his government to be a democratic yet refuses the PAM, and those who hold contrary opinion, the right of reply through the same medium. We draw your attention in support of this to two letters from employers on page 2, the contents which speak for themselves.

The public will have to wait patiently for the whole truth. In the meantime a feeling of tension and fear permeates the whole community and even the Premier himself finds it necessary to go about armed in public.

There are also reports that Government has found it necessary to arm questionable persons. As a result of this at least one incident has been reported of a gun being fired accidentally.

It is regrettable that irresponsible shooting has occurred in a peaceful community such as ours fortunately without serious injury or loss of life, but these incidents show that all is far from well in our new State.

It is high time that our Premier and other senior members of Government stay at home and work out a satisfactory solution to our problems in accordance with both the letter and spirit of our Constitution.

The Democrat also published the following:

Governor's Dep. Calls for Day of Prayer

The following is the text of a letter from His Excellency the Governor's Deputy - Mr. B. F. Dias, O.B.E., to certain Heads of Denominations and the Christian Council of Churches in the State:-

"You will of course be aware of the recent acts of violence taking place in the State and of the continued state of tension which appears to be mounting rather than abating. I am of the opinion that only the hand of Providence moved by the prayers of our citizens, can avert a great catastrophe and cause us all to search our hearts and enter upon the road of justice and love for our fellow citizens, irrespective of colour, class, creed or political persuasion. I am therefore asking all Christian Churches in the State to declare Sunday 18 June, 1967 as a National Day of Prayer when all men will kneel and ask the Almighty to grant a just peace to this troubled State."

Ronald Webster, who was at the time leading the Anguilla revolt against association with St. Kitts, wrote a book entitled *Revolutionary Leader* which was published in 2011. Webster is acclaimed in Anguilla as 'Father of the Nation' in much the same way as Robert Bradshaw is in St. Kitts. Webster says very little in his book of the events of June 10 1967 and only mentions them in passing in chapter 19 as follows:

> There was another round of discussions between the St. Kitts Government and a second delegation from Anguilla at the end of June prompted by an armed attack on St. Kitts by a group of Anguillians on June 10th, and a request by Premier Bradshaw to the Commonwealth Caribbean Governments for military assistance to end the Anguilla revolution. (page 49)

Much more is written of the events of the June 10 by the Anguillan historian Colville L. Petty and A. Nat Hodge, Anguillian journalist and editor in their book entitled *Anguilla's Battle for Freedom 1967-1969* published in 2010. In note 1 to chapter 4 headed 'Armed attack on St. Kitts' they write: 'The information in this Chapter is the result of extensive interviews with most of the men who took part in the attack on St. Kitts.' In note 2 they say 'The names of the Kittitians who were involved in the attempted coup have been withheld out of concern for their safety and that of their relatives.'

Petty and Hodge wrote:

> The notion of attacking St. Kitts was the brainchild of Ronald Webster and a prominent Kittitian lawyer. The attack was carried out on Saturday 10th June 1967. The party of armed men from Anguilla who landed in St. Kitts had two principal objectives which were interrelated. One was the defence of the Anguilla Revolution. The other was the overthrow of the government of Premier Robert Bradshaw and the installation of a government sympathetic to the Anguillian cause. Ronald Webster was fearful of an invasion from St. Kitts and reasoned that the best way of preventing it was to attack St. Kitts and overthrow its government.

Connell Harrigan, a Webster supporter, observed:

> St. Kitts was trying to get into Anguilla by fair means or by foul. We were out in the night and so forth, and we were seeing boats coming in and we figured that Bradshaw might attack us at any time, so we attacked him first.

Petty and Hodge also say that the Anguillans who attacked St. Kitts were misled into believing that there would be a general uprising in St. Kitts in support of them and were surprised when they received little support on the ground in St. Kitts. I am unable to verify any of the statements which

I have quoted from Petty and Hodge nor have any of them been proven in a court of law.

Ever since 1967 the Labour Party and its supporters have held the unshakeable perception that PAM was involved in an attempted coup of June 10, 1967. PAM and its supporters on the other hand have held the unshakeable view that Bradshaw wanted no opposition, and saw the attack from Anguilla as an opportunity to destroy PAM and sought to do so by the failed attempt of his government to prosecute some of the PAM leaders for treason. They point out that the charges were withdrawn by the government prosecutors at the trial in November 1967 details of which are discussed in a later chapter. These perceptions lie at the root of the political tribalism from which St. Kitts suffers. Until the psychological wounds of 1967 are healed, St. Kitts stands at risk of instability.

Anguilla 1967 Demonstration

PICTURE SHOWS: With British troops and police keeping things on a friendly, peaceful basis in Anguilla, members of the Black Panther organisation demonstrate against British intervention in the island. Carrying banners calling for "Solidarity with Anguilla" in London's Whitehall, they later clashed with police and several were arrested.

Anguilla – British Soldiers liming on the beach

ANGUILLA'S BATTLE FOR FREEDOM
1967 - 1969

COLVILLE L. PETTY AND A. NAT HODGE

Cover of book chronicling events in Anguilla.

4.

Nevis and the Federal Arrangements

Nevis was joined with St. Kitts and Anguilla in 1882 having previously been part of the larger Leeward Islands grouping. The government of the new colony was based in St. Kitts which was its administrative and economic hub with approximately two-thirds of the population and a strong sugar industry. Like Anguilla, Nevis was neglected by the central government in St. Kitts under the British and, after the introduction of universal adult suffrage, under the elected government. Its infrastructure was inadequate. Charlestown, its capital, became almost a ghost town as soon as businesses closed each day and, if there was a scheduled ferry service to St. Kitts, after the ferry left. The island's sugar industry had declined and many of the former sugar estates had fallen into ownership of the government but cotton was grown on some estates as a suitable replacement. Many Nevisian families had small land holdings so in that regard Nevis was very different from St. Kitts where almost all the arable land was cultivated in sugar cane. Nevisians were proud of their land ownership and, although of limited means, were proud, self-sufficient and independent people.

The people of Nevis resented the lack of infrastructure and economic opportunities in their island and the concentration of resources in St. Kitts. As happened with Anguilla, most of the infrastructure and other development in Nevis came after Nevisians gained effective control of their own affairs.However, unlike Anguilla, Nevis did not secede from St. Kitts. Political events in St. Kitts gave them that control peacefully.

By the Constitution and Elections Ordinance 1952, St. Kitts-Nevis-Anguilla was given its first legislature, the Legislative Council, to be elected under adult suffrage. It comprised ten elected members – seven from St. Kitts, two from Nevis and one from Anguilla – two nominated members and the Attorney General. The Legislative Council had power to make laws for the colony limited by the requirement of the assent of the Administrator or the Queen, with the Queen having power to withhold her assent in certain broadly defined circumstances.

Elected members from Nevis took the cause of Nevisians to the Legislature. Eugene Walwyn, a lawyer from Nevis was one such member of the 1957 Legislative Council. William Kelsick OBE was a nominated member and describes the debate in the Legislative Council on financing for Nevis in these terms:

> One of the major economic issues faced at that time, related to the fact that St. Kitts had a wage day but Nevis did not. Every week, the sugar estates in St. Kitts paid wages. However, the economic activity in Nevis was quite different. Their sugar estates had gone out of business therefore, cotton was being planted on a share basis. As a result, cotton farmers had to wait for payment which was made whenever the cotton had been sold, so many lived from one pay day to the next, sometimes under very trying circumstances because this payment would take several months. This was the pattern from as far back as the post emancipation period when the free peasantry planted cotton. Incidentally, during the 1950s, large numbers of Nevisians came to St. Kitts to work on the sugar estates so that they could have regular incomes. All of this explains why requests for subsidies for Nevis was one of the debates (sometimes quite heated) frequently held.

In the 1960s, Nevis had a secession movement which showed its political strength in a demonstration in St. Kitts organized by Nevisians who traveled to St. Kitts by boat. Bradshaw temporarily stifled the movement by cleverly enticing Eugene Walwyn to join his Labour Party government as Attorney General. Walwyn lost support in Nevis and was branded a traitor for selling out Nevis at the time of the arrangements for Associated Statehood. Walwyn went on to become a businessman, founding the Bank of Commerce in St. Kitts. He invested the Bank's money in speculative ventures including an airline. The bank went bankrupt in 1985 and many Kittitians and Nevisians lost their savings. The liquidation of Bank of Commerce has not been completed to this day. Walwyn was convicted in the High Court of fraud. He was fined $75,000.

The tragic sinking of the government owned ferry *M.V Christena* en route from St. Kitts to Nevis on August 1,1970 leaving over 230 people (the large majority Nevisians) dead, further clouded relations between St. Kitts and Nevis. In the aftermath of the disaster, caused by gross overcrowding of the vessel, the Nevis Reformation Party (NRP) was formed, with its main platform being secession from St. Kitts. Among the founders and leaders of that party was Simeon Daniel, a lawyer, who earlier in his career, worked in the civil service in St. Kitts where Bradshaw had tried unsuccessfully to court him. After Associated Statehood, Daniel returned to Nevis and immediately entered politics, becoming Chair of the Nevis Local Council and then won election to the House of Assembly in 1975 and 1980. Daniel understood and captured the spirit of Nevisians by whom he was greatly loved. He was humble and sociable and spoke in soft tones. He had a brilliant mind and was fearless.

As the other Associated States moved to full independence, St. Kitts and Nevis were delayed by the Anguilla secession issue which was not formally settled until 1980. In the latter half of the 1970s, as the NRP gained strength, Nevisians began to agitate more strongly for secession. An unofficial referendum was held in 1977 and resulted in 99 per cent of the votes cast in favour of secession.

Bradshaw died in 1978 and Southwell in 1979 leaving the Labour Party under the leadership of Lee Moore. Moore was a brilliant advocate and a man of integrity but not a great politician. His short temper in the face of political rhetoric did not help. Soon after he took office as Premier he upset members of the civil service by assembling them in a hall and reminding them of their responsibilities and what it meant to be a civil servant. He refused to call a meeting of the House of Assembly after Kennedy Simmonds of PAM won the by-election for the Central Basseterre seat which Bradshaw had held up to his death. It took a court case for that election to be finally determined. The returning officer rejected 99 ballots and declared the Labour Party candidate Anthony Ribeiro duly elected. Simmonds took the matter to the High Court. The Judge counted the ballots himself and declared Simmonds the winner by 22 votes. The Court of Appeal upheld the Judge's decision on August 10, 1979.

Rather than calling a meeting of the National Assembly and allowing Simmonds to be sworn in, Moore decided to call a general election. That election was held on February 18, 1980. Of the seven seats that were up for grabs in St. Kitts and the two in Nevis, Moore's Labour Party won four seats in St. Kitts and PAM, led by Simmonds, won three. NRP won the two seats in Nevis and joined PAM to form the government with Simmonds as Premier and Daniel as Minister of Finance. With his party holding the balance of power and in control of the key Ministry, Daniel temporarily shelved his secessionist agenda and focused his attention on redressing the perceived wrongs done to Nevis in the past. His colleague, Ivor Stevens, the other elected representative of NRP, joined Daniel in the Simmonds-led government as Minister of Communications and Works, another key ministry from which to redress the imbalance from which Nevis had suffered.

With the Anguilla situation resolved and Nevis secession put on hold, the way was now open for St. Kitts and Nevis to move to independence following the other Associated States of Grenada in 1974, Dominica in 1978, St. Lucia and St. Vincent and the Grenadines in 1979 and Antigua and Barbuda in 1981. The most controversial issue in the debate on the independence constitution was the relationship between St. Kitts and Nevis. Leveraging the balance of power which NRP held, Nevis ensured that it got effective control of its own affairs. The system chosen by the government of the day was that of a Federation but a very unusual one. Nevis was to have its own government but St. Kitts was not to have its own government. There was to be a Federal government, with elected representatives from both islands. The Federal government would administer St. Kitts. To borrow the terminology of the Phillips Commission, Nevis was to be federated with St. Kitts and Nevis. That arrangement would create the possibility (as happened in 1993 and again in 2015) of Nevis holding the balance of power in the Federal Parliament while controlling its own internal affairs.

The Nevisians went further by insisting on the inclusion of a secession clause and also that any amendments to several key provisions of the constitution would require a two thirds vote in St. Kitts and a separate two thirds vote in Nevis. Nevis was to have a Premier and Cabinet called the Nevis Island Administration and its own legislature called the Nevis Island Assembly.

Those proposals were met with great furore in St. Kitts causing the opposition Labour Party to boycott the constitutional conference. However,the British succumbed to the government proposals and St. Kitts and Nevis got its strange Federation on September 19, 1983.

Within the 1980s, skillfully led by Simeon Daniel, who was made a National Hero after his death in 2012, Nevis advanced beyond recognition. In the first post- independence election in 1984, PAM won six of the eight seats in St. Kitts, giving them a majority of the eleven seats in the National Assembly. This meant that they did not need the support of the NRP to run the Federal government. However, Nevis and the NRP remained in the Federal government. Daniel gave up the Ministry of Finance and took a less important ministry which freed him up to undertake his responsibilities as the first Premier of Nevis. Ivor Stevens, Daniel's NRP colleague, remained actively involved in the Federal Government as Minister responsible for Communications and Works, still a key ministry as far as Nevis was concerned.

Despite the favourable effect for Nevis of the new constitutional arrangements, secession was by no means a dead issue. The secession clause 113 was invoked by the Nevis Island Assembly in 1997, by which time NRP had lost power in Nevis in 1992 to the Concerned Citizens Movement (CCM) led by Vance Amory and PAM had lost power in St. Kitts in 1995 to the Labour Party led by Denzil Douglas. The catalysts for the referendum on secession were the financial arrangements between St. Kitts and Nevis and the implications for Nevis of external affairs falling unconditionally under the control of the Federal government. These had been issues even when PAM and NRP were in a coalition. Tensions grew after NRP lost power in Nevis and after PAM lost power in St. Kitts.

The financial arrangements in the constitution were different to the political ones, most importantly taxation which was a Federal matter. The Nevis Island Assembly had very limited power of taxation as it could not tax profits or income or property or imports or exports. The revenue sharing arrangements were very simple; taxation revenue was to be shared on a per capita basis and in that accounting Nevis was to be assessed for its share of common services and debt.

There were however practical aspects of this arrangement that were abused by successive Federal governments to the annoyance of Nevisians, especially the fact that most of the taxation revenue was received by the Federal government in St. Kitts. Equally irksome to Nevisians was the fact that the Federal government had control over external affairs which meant that when Nevis borrowed from overseas requiring a guarantee, only the Federal government could issue such a guarantee. Nevis also has to rely on the goodwill of the Federal government to share in aid from foreign governments. Until 2015 when Mark Brantley became Minister of Foreign Affairs in the Federal Government while retaining the position of Deputy Premier, Nevis had no formal direct contact with such governments. Nevisians also claimed that they were ignored in appointments for diplomatic and external representative positions. At times their leaders were not included in teams representing the country at regional and international fora. Given the importance of foreign direct investment to the island's economic development, the NIA regarded that as a deliberate attempt by the Federal government to stymie important opportunities for exposure of the NIA to sources of investment capital. St. Kitts and Nevis often competed for such capital.

The operation of any money sharing arrangement whether it is within a family or a business or a government is dependent in large measure on the honesty and goodwill of the parties involved and their willingness to compromise. Even if you write in greatest detail the rules applicable to this type of arrangement the parties can still disagree if they want to. The lack of communication and compromise between the leaders in St. Kitts and those in Nevis over the operation of the financial arrangements re-opened the mistrust between the islands.

The Federal election of 1993 had brought another PAM/NRP government but this time a minority one with PAM/NRP holding 5 seats, Labour 4 and CCM 2. Violence erupted and a state of emergency was briefly declared. Tensions continued until November 1994 when the Four Seasons Accord was made. That agreement resulted from a meeting at the Four Seasons Hotel in Nevis attended by the leaders of all political parties in the country, leaders of the private sector, Church organizations and other civil society bodies. An outside date of November 15, 1995 was set for the next election. Various other arrangements were made with a view to improving the governance of the country. The full text of the Accord is set out in an appendix to this book.

The Labour Party won power with an overwhelming majority in the National Assembly in the general election of July 1995. The party had maintained its vehement opposition to the Federal arrangements but said in its manifesto for the election that it wanted unity among the people and pledged that within the first 100 days of forming the government a constitutional reform conference would be convened to serve as a springboard for the decision on substantial constitutional reform for St. Kitts and Nevis. Those pledges reflected the very clear position of the Labour Party both before and after independence that the current constitutional arrangements established on independence were unfair.

However, before the new Labour government could act on its manifesto promises, Amory jumped the gun when in April 1996, the NIA appointed a Constitutional Advisory (Review) Committee with the following terms of reference:

- to hold public meetings throughout Nevis and invite all shades of public opinion on the constitution;

- to examine and assess the constitution as it relates to St. Kitts and Nevis;

- to advise the Administration of what changes (if any) should be made to the constitution;

- to advise the Administration whether a new constitution should be drafted to govern the relationship between St. Kitts and Nevis.

In its report the Phillips Commission, appointed by the Federal government, stated that the NIA appointed Constitutional Advisory (Review) Committee had noted the following trends:

"(a) The current constitution was originally intended to cover a three-year term. This has not (until now) been officially reviewed. It was therefore considered timely and appropriate to have the constitutional arrangements between St. Kitts and Nevis reviewed with the objective of correcting any obvious abnormalities.

(b) The majority of the persons interviewed felt that separate (local) governments for St. Kitts and Nevis should be considered with some type of "Treaty" arrangement put in place to govern areas of common interest like international trade, defence and foreign representation.

(c) It was considered important to maintain an amicable working relationship between both governments to facilitate free movement of nationals, goods and common services.

(d) As an alternative to the current constitutional arrangement a revised model was recommended which essentially advocates two separate Assemblies for St. Kitts and Nevis. This model would see all laws specifically affecting Nevis being passed in the Nevis House of Assembly, and laws specifically affecting St. Kitts being passed in the St. Kitts House of Assembly. The Assembly of one country (sic) would have no jurisdiction over the other. Elections to the first and subsequent local assembly (sic) under this arrangement (would) be held on a predetermined date every five years in both islands. A Federal Assembly (would) comprise an equal number of representatives from both local Assemblies. This Federal Assembly (would) "rubber stamp" laws passed in both Assemblies and (would) exercise jurisdiction over Federal matters like defence, foreign borrowing, foreign representation and the like. The Federal Assembly would be headed by a Prime Minister. This position would be rotated between the Premiers of St. Kitts and Nevis every five years. The Federal Assembly would be supported financially by both islands, using criteria other than population as the basis. Eventually, this would translate into some type of confederation between the two islands.

(e) A Federal Public Service Commission would comprise representatives of autonomous bodies in St. Kitts and Nevis, with the Chairman of the Nevis Public Service Commission serving as ex-officio and vice versa, to deal with transfers at the Federal level and other related matters.

(f) It was recommended that Clause 27 in the current constitution be eliminated."

The NIA Review committee was not allowed to complete its work as, in June 1996, Amory announced that he was moving immediately for secession and in July 1996 introduced a Separation Bill in the Nevis Assembly. The Assembly members from the opposition NIA absented themselves from the sitting at which the second and third readings of the Separation Bill were tabled in November 1996. The Bill could not therefore receive the required two thirds majority of all elected members of the Assembly.

Amory then decided to call an election with his CCM party campaigning on a secession platform. In the election held on February 24, 1997 CCM won three of the five seats with NRP winning the other two. Shortly after, in April 1997 Amory again moved a motion in the Assembly for secession. The Separation Bill was unanimously passed on October 13, 1997 with NRP deciding it would leave the matter for decision by the people of Nevis. The next step required by the constitution was a referendum of

Nevis voters. For secession to take effect a two thirds majority of all votes cast was required.

On December 15, 1997 the Federal Government appointed a Constitutional Commission headed by Sir Fred Phillips, the first Governor of the Associated State of St. Kitts-Nevis-Anguilla. By then Sir Fred had long left St. Kitts and returned to private practice of the law through which he had earned an excellent reputation as a regionalist and a constitutional lawyer. The other commissioners were Kenneth Rattray Q.C. from Jamaica and Reginald Dumas from Trinidad and Tobago. The terms of reference of the Phillips Commission were:

- to consider whether the provisions of the 1983 Independence Constitution are such as to give expression to the normal relations between one unit of a federal entity and another;

- to review the existing constitutional arrangements in the country and to make recommendations as to the nature of any reforms deemed expedient; and

- in particular, to examine all practicable bases of future relations between St. Kitts and Nevis, including that of separation under section 113 of the Constitution.

Between January and July 1998 the Phillips Commission held several public meetings in St. Kitts and one in Nevis. A second meeting scheduled for Nevis was (according to the Report) cancelled at the last moment by the Nevis organisers.

The Phillips Commission also visited the Virgin Islands, the United Kingdom, The United States of America and Canada where they consulted with Kittitians and Nevisians, government representatives and with national and international organisations.

Not surprisingly, the CCM, more concerned with its campaign for secession, refused to participate in the deliberations of the Commission whose report was presented to the Governor General on July 31, 1998.

The referendum on secession was held in Nevis on August 10,1998. A total of 2,427 or 61.83 per cent of those who voted did so in favour of secession while 1,498 or 38.17 per cent of the voters voted against secession. The 61.83 per cent vote in favour fell just short of the two thirds majority required by the constitution for the secession resolution to succeed.

In light of the findings of the Phillips Report and the results of the Nevis referendum, the Federal government decided to supplement the process of the Philips Commission and in January 1999 appointed a Task Force on Constitutional Reform again headed by Sir Fred Phillips. The Task Force had a wider composition than the Phillips Commission, comprising Sir Fred along with Brynmor Pollard SC, Reginald Dumas, Cedric Harper and Professor Simon Jones-Hendrickson. The last two named are St. Kitts and Nevis nationals both distinguished in higher education, Harper at The University of The West Indies, Mona Campus, Jamaica and Jones-Hendrickson at the University of The Virgin Islands. Like the Commission, the Task Force consulted widely. It reported on July 25, 1999. The recommendations of the Commission and the Task Force on the future relations between St. Kitts and Nevis are almost identical.

Before giving the details of the recommendations I set out two extracts from the Report of the Phillips Task Force. The Task Force began the chapter of its report on the relationship between St. Kitts and Nevis with this statement:

> We begin by saying that among the people we spoke to and heard from, publicly and privately, in St. Kitts and Nevis during the last four months, we found overwhelming support for the continuation of the two islands as one state. Various suggestions were made on the nature and governance of that state, but the principle of oneness was almost universally accepted and supported.

The second extract is from paragraph nine of the chapter referred to of the Task Force report:

> It was represented to us that the official and institutional relationship between St. Kitts and Nevis left a great deal to be desired. We were told often that it was the politicians in both islands who were the problem, the implication being that that they were out of step with the rest of the community. One wonders, if that were indeed so, why has not the rest of the community which elects the politicians, imposed its wishes on them.

One would have hoped that with local representation on the Task Force, Messrs Harper and Jones-Hendrickson would have provided some answer to the question. My own view is that too many persons in the rest of the community were and still are, inflicted with polarization, do not think for themselves and simply play 'follow the leader'. The politicians have little fear therefore that the community will impose its will on them and merrily go along playing their games.

It is worthy of note at this point that the Task Force met with the leaders of the main political parties and held private and public meetings on both islands including five public meetings on Nevis and a call-in discussion on *VON Radio*, a popular Nevis based radio station. They were received by Premier Amory and the Report quotes him as saying that it remained the views of the CCM (after the referendum) that the interest of the people of Nevis can only be best achieved by constitutional separation from St. Kitts but 'we are prepared to work within a framework of constitutional reform, provided only that that is indeed the will of the people of Nevis.'

In the 17 years since the referendum there have been substantial improvements in business relations and in communication by travel and telecommunications between St. Kitts and Nevis and therefore much greater movement of people and contact between them. Social media has created a greater bond between young people. Even though it may not have left Amory's mind, one hardly hears talk of secession these days. The NRP is now firmly aligned with the Labour Party so one would not expect them (at least not while that alliance remains) to support secession. The 2015 election has brought a novel change to the party dynamics as for the first time CCM, having joined the Team Unity alliance, are part of the Federal executive with Amory and Brantley now Federal ministers as well as Premier and Deputy Premier respectively of Nevis. Team Unity says it is committed to a review of the constitution, although one never knows what might happen with politicians. In any event, it would be useful to look at a summary of the Phillips Commission and Task Force proposals.

They recommended that:

- St. Kitts should have its own legislature with power to legislate on all matters for St. Kitts other than those allocated to the Federal Parliament (see below for those powers).

- Nevis should retain its own legislature with power to legislate on all matters for Nevis other than those allocated to the Federal Parliament.

- St. Kitts should have its own executive branch in the form of a Cabinet headed by a Premier and four or five Ministers.

- Nevis should retain its Cabinet with a Premier and two or three Ministers.

- The Ministers in each Cabinet should be appointed by the Premier from within or outside the island legislature and be subject to confirmation by the island legislature.

- There should be a Federal Parliament comprising equal numbers of elected members from St. Kitts and Nevis and non-voting independent members appointed by the President after consultation.

- The Federal Parliament should have power to legislate on matters of national security (including defence), foreign affairs and the judiciary.

- A seventy per cent majority of all elected members should be required to pass legislation in the Federal Parliament.

- The Head of State should be a President responsible for national security (including defence), foreign affairs and the judiciary subject to parliamentary oversight via national security and foreign affairs committees.

- The President should also have power to make appointments to sensitive positions subject to confirmation by Parliament.

- The Presidency should be rotated between Nevis and St. Kitts beginning with St. Kitts. A person would be qualified to be the President from St. Kitts or Nevis if he were born on the island or one of his or her parents was born on the island.

- The term of office of the President should be five years

- When a President is to be elected the two island legislatures should consult and agree on the nomination of two qualified persons to be put before the electorate for election. The electorate on both islands should vote between the persons nominated to elect a President.

- There should be a Vice President. The Vice President should come from the other island to the President. The Vice President should be nominated and elected in the same manner as the President.

- The President and Vice President should be able to serve a second term although of course not consecutively.

- The President should appoint two Secretaries of State from outside the legislatures and Parliament who would function as his Cabinet.

The recommendations address the major issues of concern to all the parties. They give St. Kitts a separate government and they give Nevis greater control over taxation in Nevis and a say in security and foreign affairs thus providing a fair and balanced basis for a resumption of the discussion. Some may think that they are complicated and that it would be costly for a small country such as ours to add a third tier of government to the two we already have. My view is that it would be worth the cost if it would create stability and end the bickering and lingering resentment.

The Phillips Commission also addressed the important matter of dispute resolution. Again, given human nature and the nature of politics and given the St. Kitts and Nevis experience, it would be wise to have a formal dispute resolution process with recourse through the courts as a last resort. The mechanisms recommended by the Task Force are firstly a Conciliation Committee of the Federal Parliament, then if not resolved to mediation by a permanent group of facilitators chosen from nationals of Caricom by the Federal government and the island governments. The Conciliation Committee should then seek to resolve the dispute based on the recommendations of the mediation group. If they fail then the dispute should be resolved by decision on a vote of seventy per cent of the Conciliation Committee, that decision to be binding. The recommended composition of the Conciliation Committee was three members from Nevis and five from St. Kitts.

As to the famous secession clause 113 of the constitution, the Commission and the Task Force recommended a 'sunset' clause that is a fixed period of time after which the right to secession for Nevis would expire.

The wide differences over the constitutional arrangements between St. Kitts and Nevis remain unresolved and ripe for any politician, of any side, who wants to use these disputes for political ends. This issue should be re-opened and can with goodwill on all sides be resolved. St. Kitts and Nevis will then have one less factor contributing to our brooding democracy. The 26 Month Election has provided another opportunity for this.

I am ever mindful that any change to the arrangements between St. Kitts and Nevis will require separate two thirds majorities in the Federal Assembly and in the Nevis Island Assembly and two thirds majorities in separate referenda in St. Kitts and Nevis. That is a tall order. It will require a complete change in political culture on both islands from tribal to issue based politics. As difficult as that will be to achieve and as long as it may take, those who promote the change should not be deterred and should continue the debate.

Simeon Daniel, being sworn in as Premier of the NIA.
Courtesy of The National Archives, St. Kitts.

CCM wins Local Govt in Nevis, 1992. (L-R) Vance Amory, Leonard Small, Franklin Brand, Colin Tyrell, Malcolm Guishard. Courtesy of The National Archives, St. Kitts

*Prime Minister Simmonds (L) and Nevis Premier Amory.
Courtesy of The National Archives, St. Kitts*

Team Unity member Mark Brantley interacting with school children on his way to Parliament

Waterfront, Charlestown, Nevis

Turtle Beach, St.Kitts with Nevis in the background.

5.   *The Rule of Law*

The primary lesson that I take from the events of the 26 Month Election is that we have seen first hand that in an 'elective dictatorship' (a term coined by the late Simeon McIntosh former law Professor of the University of the West Indies) such as ours the rule of law can be overcome by the rule of man if the people are not vigilant. That nearly happened in St. Kitts and Nevis. It is the primary lesson because had it happened, none of the other lessons would have mattered. There are many steps that can be taken to deter that in future and one that should be taken immediately is a constitutional amendment to impose term limits on the prime minister. Reform of the governance laws is also required to promote greater transparency and disclosure of information and to make public officials more accountable. I will address these issues of reform in a later chapter but in this chapter I will focus on the rule of law and its importance.

From time immemorial there has been a distinction between the rule of law and the rule of man in the governance of nations. The rule of law applies where there is a democratic system for the making of laws; checks and balances on those who are elected or otherwise exercise power; an independent judicial system; accountability and transparency in public affairs; equality before the law and where no man is above the law. The rule of man applies where a man who is above the law governs and can make the law and/or apply it or control its application as he decides without effective recourse by the governed. In ancient days the rule of man was the prevailing system with nations governed or controlled absolutely by kings, chiefs, emperors, dictators, demagogues or despots. But even in those days the rule of law applied in some forms. Three centuries before Christ the famous Greek philosopher Aristotle expressed a preference for the rule of law in these words 'the rule of law…is preferable to that of any individual' and 'For in democracies where the laws are not supreme demagogues spring up'. A century before Christ the famous

Roman statesman Cicero did likewise saying 'We are all servants of the law that we may be free'.

In modern days the rule of law is regarded as the norm. It is described as the bedrock of democracy and its effectiveness is usually a measure of economic development particularly in developing countries. The United Nations expounds in great measure on the rule of law and expects its application from member states. But that is not always the case as many countries, while holding themselves out as constitutional democracies or while having the infrastructure for the rule of law, still suffer from the rule of man.

Why is this so? I believe that despite the improvement in the human physical condition caused by advances in science, technology and education and despite greater political and social consciousness, human nature basically remains the same; and despite the preachings of Christ man is still too often motivated by love of power, greed, hatred, arrogance, egotism and jealousy as opposed to the values that Christ preached of love, tolerance, forgiveness and humility. Their negative traits often override their good qualities and drive men in a quest for absolute power and dominance over their own people. And we know what Abraham Lincoln said on the subject:

> Nearly all men can stand adversity, but if you want to test a man's character, give him power.

History is replete with examples of countries that have, due to the dominant traits of the leader, descended from the rule of law to the rule of man. And in nearly all of those cases persons within the country, driven by the same negative traits, have for personal gain supported the resulting tyranny.

It is instructive to look at South Africa under Nelson Mandela and Zimbabwe under Robert Mugabe. Mandela and Mugabe were both freedom fighters for just causes, both endured lengthy imprisonment for their causes, both triumphed over their oppressors and both were elected to the highest office of their country on a platform of reconciliation and equality. But there the similarities end. Mandela applied his beliefs by forming a government of national unity with one of his former oppressors F.W. DeKlerk as his senior vice- president. He established a Truth and Reconciliation Commission to promote forgiveness and healing, began the fight to redress the economic imbalance created by the evil apartheid system and sought no major personal gain - readily admitting his own imperfections and was the epitome of humility. He served only one term as President and flatly refused a second. On the other hand shortly after taking power Mugabe turned on his own black people as well as the former white oppressors. Forty-five years later he is still in power at an age in excess of 90 and apparently not intent on leaving office anytime soon. He has created extraordinary wealth for himself, his family and elite hangers-on while the vast majority of his people suffer untold hardship. Having begun as the freedom fighter he has become the oppressor.

US President Barak Obama hit the nail on the head at the memorial service for Mandela when he said:

> There are too many leaders who claim solidarity with Madiba's struggle for freedom, but do not tolerate dissent from their own people. And there are too many of us who stand on the sidelines, comfortable in complacency or cynicism when our voices must be heard.

You may well ask what about St. Kitts and Nevis; does the rule of law apply here? We have a constitution that protects fundamental rights, an independent and accessible court system, and an elected legislature and some, albeit minimal, checks and balances on the use of executive power. These are some essential features of the rule of law. However, our system displays serious shortcomings in the woeful inadequacy of the checks and balances on executive power, our porous electoral laws and the lack of campaign finance legislation. By international standards we can, on balance claim to be governed by the rule of law but this cannot be taken for granted. A constitution and laws do not alone guarantee the maintenance of the rule of law. As important are the attitudes of those in leadership and of the people, to the constitution and laws and to each other. A people who do not respect the constitution and laws invite descent into the rule of man. A people who do not guard and exercise their rights stand vulnerable to lose them. So it is up to all of us citizens to determine whether we will maintain and improve the rule of law.

How then do we the people of St. Kitts and Nevis currently stand as a nation in our attitudes to the rule of law? Not very well I must say. A good reference point is the preamble to the constitution which is rarely publicly discussed. I assume that is because it is not controversial. The preamble is meant to express what we stand for as a nation. It says:

"WHEREAS the People of Saint Christopher and Nevis –

declare that the nation is established on the belief in Almighty God and the inherent dignity of each individual; assert that they are entitled to the protection of fundamental rights and freedoms; believe in the concept of true democracy with free and fair elections; desire the creation of a climate of economic wellbeing in the context of respect for law and order; and are committed to achieve their national objectives with a unity of purpose;…."

My views are:-

- We declare that our nation is established on the belief in Almighty God but too many, on all sides, put political party above all else and regard their party leaders as superhuman. They in turn can never admit fault.

- We declare that our nation is established on the belief in the inherent dignity of each individual but those of the opposite party are called hogs and dogs. We assert that we are entitled to the protection of fundamental rights and freedoms. Those rights include the right to political opinions but those with opposing opinions should not thrive.

- We claim to believe in the concept of true democracy with free and fair elections but many will do whatever they have to for the election of their party. We are committed to achieve our national objectives with a unity of purpose but in practice there couldn't be more disunity which clouds our national objectives.

- We need as a nation a new paradigm of respect, tolerance, civility and maturity and a new political culture. We need as a people to practice what the preamble to our constitution says and foster and promote the rule of law. Our leaders should by their actions, as well as talk, lead the way in reaffirming the principles expressed in the preamble and in following the letter and spirit of the constitution. Only then will there be a new and salutary phase of our history. Then too the likelihood of St. Kitts and Nevis descending into the rule of man will be reduced.

Independence Ceremony Warner Park including Princess Margaret.
Courtesy of the National Archives, St. Kitts

1982 Labour Party Demonstration against Independence White Paper.
Courtesy of The National Archives St. Kitts

PART TWO

In the Aftermath of the 26 Month Election: Reflections on our Legal Systems, the Constitution, Governance and the Society

View over the south-east peninsula of St. Kitts, towards Nevis. Courtesy of Chazzette Mills

Caribbean Court of Justice, Port of Spain, Trinidad. Caribbeannewsservice.com photo

6. *The Legal System*

The West Indies Associated States Supreme Court was established on February 27, 1967 simultaneously with the grant of Associated Statehood to St. Kitts-Nevis-Anguilla. Its jurisdiction covered Antigua, Dominica, Grenada, St. Kitts-Nevis-Anguilla, St. Lucia and St. Vincent. The jurisdiction was extended to the colonies of Montserrat and the British Virgin Islands and (after its separation in 1980) Anguilla.

The court was created with two divisions. The High Court sits on an ongoing basis in each island with one or more resident judges. The Court of Appeal, based in St. Lucia, exercises an appellate jurisdiction and sits in each country at fixed times in each year. As the Associated States gained independence the name of the court was changed to the Eastern Caribbean Supreme Court which remains today as the court of first instance and the first appellate court. The final appellate court for St. Kitts and Nevis has remained the Privy Council in London despite the establishment of the Caribbean Court of Justice (CCJ), more on which will be said later.

Because of the usually overlapping nature of the legislature and the executive, the courts play an even more significant role in our system and their independence is critical to our democracy. They function as guardians of the constitution and the fundamental rights of the citizen and as the arbiter of legal disputes. Their power is intended to deter abuse by, and keep the powerful executive in compliance with the constitution and the laws. Thankfully the British saw the wisdom of creating a regional court rather than a separate court system for each island. I hate to think what would have happened in 1967 or in 2012-15 if St. Kitts and Nevis had a separate court with the government exercising influence on the appointment of judges.

The first real test of the new West Indies Associated States Supreme Court came in St. Kitts within six months of its establishment. The test came in the form of the legal objections to the detention in prison of opponents of the government under the state of emergency and the trials of those charged with offences arising out of the events of June 10, 1967.

Applications were made by way *of habeas corpus* by Dr. William Herbert, Leader of the Peoples Action Movement (detained on June 10 1967) and Mr. Henry Charles (detained on June 14, 1967) for their release from detention under the state of emergency on the ground that their detention was a breach of their fundamental right to personal freedom and therefore unlawful. The High Court judge dismissed the applications, but on August 10, 1967 the Court of Appeal found their detention to be unconstitutional and ordered their release.

Then came the criminal trials in October and November. The accused in the first and second cases, charged with shooting at police officers, were acquitted by the jury. The third case, known as the treason case, involved seven persons accused of conspiracy to overthrow the lawful government of the State. The accused included Dr. Herbert and Michael Powell who was to become in 1983 the first Deputy Prime Minister of independent St. Kitts and Nevis.

On November 14, 1967, following the acquittal in the second trial and just before the commencement of the treason case, the House of Assembly unanimously passed a resolution as follows:

> Be it resolved that this House expresses its complete lack of confidence in the administration of justice as applied to this Associated State under the present Constitution and supports such action as Government may take to…inquire carefully into ways and means by which the existing Supreme Court Order, including the Agreement, can be amended to ensure that the rule of law is impartially observed.

The Labour Spokesman, newspaper mouthpiece of the Bradshaw-led ruling Labour Party, on the following day, referred to the resolution as historic. Then on November 20, 1967 before the treason trial began the Chief Justice Sir Allen Lewis convened the court in Basseterre and made a statement the first part of which is reproduced in full:

> • The attention of the Court has been drawn to a resolution passed in the House of Assembly expressing lack of confidence in the administration of justice in this State, and also to the debate which took place on that resolution and was broadcast over the St. Kitts radio station.

- The Court recognizes the right of the Legislature to entertain and debate resolutions, but deplores the fact that Government should have introduced this resolution into the House in the midst of a series of trials of persons accused upon charges alleged to be concerned with an attempt to overthrow the existing Government and immediately before the commencement of the trial of the most important of the charges, namely, conspiracy to overthrow the Government.

- The Court must take note of the fact that these trials are in sense political trials, a leading member of the Opposition Party being the central figure, and that the introduction of the resolution and the debate in the House follow immediately upon verdicts of acquittal by the jury in the first two of the trials.

- The Court deprecates the fact that in these circumstances the debate was used by Ministers of Government for the purpose of criticizing the conduct of the two trials by the trial judge and of impeaching his integrity, no other reason being stated but that of the Government's dissatisfaction with certain rulings made by the trial judge and comments by him in the course of his summings up.

- The Court takes note of the fact that during the debate statements relating to the subject matter of the pending conspiracy charge were read out. This conduct tends to prejudice the fair trial of the accused and constitutes a contempt of court. This course of action was pursued notwithstanding a written request from the Chief Justice to the Premier that while the trials were pending the radio station should abstain from broadcasts which might tend to prejudice the fair trial of the accused.

- The Court is not concerned with the opinions expressed during the debate as to the status of the House except to say that they were very misleading and display a complete misunderstanding of the respective status of the House and of the Supreme Court under the Constitution of this State.

The Chief Justice then went on to relate the facts including

- some five hours after the verdict of acquittal in the first trial was returned, an illegal demonstration of disorderly persons was staged outside the hotel at which the trial judge (Mr. Justice St. Bernard) was residing, protesting that the judge was biased;

- the Chief Justice immediately visited St. Kitts and inquired from the Government whether it had any information suggesting that the trial judge might have a special interest in leaning in favour of the accused or against the Crown and was informed that Government had none and was not impeaching the personal integrity of the trial judge;

- between the first and second trials the judge was threatened by telephone and by letter;

- during the second trial two jurors received threatening letters which included a threat on the life of the judge;

- two requests by the Chief Justice that an official appeal should be made to the public over the St. Kitts radio station not to interfere with the trials went unheeded;

- immediately after the accused in the second trial were acquitted Premier Bradshaw telephoned the Chief Justice and requested the immediate removal from the State of the trial judge;

- Mr. Justice St. Bernard asked to be relieved of presiding over the remaining trials for personal reasons and was replaced by Mr. Justice Bishop.

The statement of the Chief Justice ended as follows:

> While the Supreme Court is an essential part of the structure of Government established by the Constitution of this State, it is constitutionally independent of the Executive and the Legislature. Its judges take no side in disputes, political, personal or otherwise. They will continue to administer justice according to law to all persons, fearlessly and with impartiality, and in accordance with the oaths which they have taken.

> This Statement is made with the approval of all the judges of the High Court and of the Court of Appeal.

The treason trial began the same day but a week later the prosecution informed the court that it was offering no further evidence against any of the accused who were then acquitted. The fourth and fifth cases against Herbert and Powell respectively were likewise disposed of.

The government then publicly circulated a handbill in which, attempting to justify the decision of the prosecution to discontinue the case, it said it was clear that the jury would not acquit any of the accused. It said that the trials were being used for political propaganda and outside lawyers had come in and used the court to launch vicious political attacks on the government. The government said it would establish a Commission of Inquiry into the events of June 10, 1967.

The large prosecution team led by Fred Wills QC of Guyana included the Director of Public Prosecutions, the late Joseph Archibald QC, a national of St. Kitts and Nevis. After the trials, Dr. Archibald left St. Kitts; his loss to St. Kitts and Nevis was the gain of the British Virgin Islands (BVI) and the region as a whole. From his new base in the BVI Dr. Archibald embarked on a distinguished and influential legal career which continued until his death in April 2014. He served in many capacities including Barrister-at –law and Queens Counsel, jurist and judge. He was the mover behind the creation of the OECS Bar Association and played an important role in the establishment of the Caribbean Court of Justice (CCJ.)

It is worthy of note also that lawyers came to St. Kitts from all over the Caribbean to join local lawyers in representing the detainees and the accused in the trials. They included Lloyd Luckoo QC of Guyana, Malcolm Butt QC and Karl Hudson Phillips of Trinidad, Dudley Thompson and Lloyd Barnett of Jamaica, Bernard St. John and Jack Dear of Barbados and Jenner Armour of Dominica. Local lawyers included Sir Maurice Davis, later QC and Chief Justice of the Eastern Caribbean Supreme Court, Frank Henville QC and Fred Kelsick, later QC. These lawyers all had or went on to distinguished careers in the law and were recognized for such in the region.

A headline on the front page of *The Labour Spokesman* of October 7, 1967 said ***Why are they bringing in 20 Lawyers from Abroad? An effort to in fluence the court.***

On November 15, 1967, John Kelsick, one of the defence lawyers then practicing in St. Kitts, was deported to his native Montserrat based on a statement critical of the government he was alleged to have made socially to another lawyer connected with the government. On November 21 Jack Dear, another of the defence lawyers, was declared an undesirable visitor.

Lawyers from the region have over the years continued to appear in the courts of St. Kitts and Nevis when litigation has been needed to defend the rights of citizens or to fight the abuse of government power. Douglas Mendes SC and Christopher Hamel Smith SC, both of Trinidad, led the case for the opposition in the MONC claim and the Boundaries cases referred to in the chronology of the events of the 26 Month Election. Long may that trend continue.

The litigation arising from the events of 1967 continued until 1979. John Reynolds, one of the detainees, sued the government in 1968 for damages for his wrongful detention. In July 1967 the government lawyers had told the tribunal appointed to consider the evidence against the detainees that the government had no evidence against Mr. Reynolds. Despite this, the government kept him detained until August 10, 1967 when he was released with the other detainees following the judgment of the Court of Appeal referred to above. Reynolds continued his suit into the 1970s and was awarded exemplary damages by the Court of Appeal although the total sum awarded him of $18,000 was surprisingly miniscule.

The government had tried to avoid any liability for the wrongful detention of the individuals by passing an Indemnity Act. That contemptuous piece of legislation was given short thrift and struck down as unconstitutional by the High Court, the Court of Appeal and the Privy Council which ended the matter when the Government appealed against the damages awarded to Mr. Reynolds. In 1979 the Privy Council upheld the damages awarded to him by the Court of Appeal.

The abuse of the fundamental rights of Reynolds, the disrespect for and attack on the court and the attempt to cover their unlawful deeds by the diabolical Indemnity Act show that in times of political tension politicians, who might in normal times respect the separation of powers and the independence of the judiciary, can easily lose that respect. All the more reason why we need strong courts.

The St. Kitts and Nevis constitution contemplates in section 38 the move from the Privy Council to a regional court as the country's final court of appeal. The establishment of a final regional court was debated over many years. In 2001 the Caribbean Court of Justice (CCJ) was established by agreement between Caricom countries who agreed to fund it by capital contributions up front to a trust fund via the Caribbean Development Bank. This method of funding made sense as the governments did not trust each other (and very few people would have trusted them) to fund the court by periodic contributions. The way that successive governments of Trinidad and Tobago have changed position justifies the trust deficit.

The CCJ has an original jurisdiction to hear disputes under the Caricom Treaty. All Caricom members are subject to this jurisdiction. The CCJ also has an appellate jurisdiction, the intention of the founders being that all English speaking Caricom member countries would make the court their final court of appeal to replace the Privy Council in London. This step was seen as the final act of independence of the countries and as completing the repatriation from Britain of their sovereignty. However, despite all founder countries contributing financially to the Court, only four members of Caricom – Barbados, Guyana and Belize and very lately Dominica - have, as at May 2015, acceded to its appellate jurisdiction. The other English speaking member countries continue to cling to the British apron strings. Even Trinidad and Tobago which provides the headquarters of the court has not acceded to its appellate jurisdiction.

The British Government has told the regional governments nicely that it would be happy if they would complete the repatriation of their sovereignty and it will not continue indefinitely to fund the Privy Council as their final court. Why then you might ask would governments so hooked on sovereignty not accept their own court for which they (or more correctly their taxpayers) pay? The immediate stimulus for the establishment of the CCJ to replace the Privy Council was said to be that the Privy Council opposes and was making it difficult for enforcement of the death penalty. Another good reason to establish our own court. Why then the delay? A reason put forward for the delay is that some of the countries need approval by referendum to change their constitutions to replace the Privy Council with the CCJ. Some politicians are uncomfortable with that as a referendum is a good opportunity for the people to embarrass a sitting government as happened in St. Vincent and the Grenadines. But what about those countries, like St. Kitts and Nevis, which do not need a referendum? The excuse for their delay has been that all OECS countries wanted to join the CCJ at the same time. That in my opinion is not the real reason.

The real reason is that the reticent governments wanted before joining to see how strong the CCJ would be in holding governments to proper governance. They were worried that the Privy Council was becoming too intrusive as in the Barbados case of *Williams v Blackman* where the Privy Council held in 1994 that the court could review a Cabinet decision to award a large government contract made under a statutory power. They were also concerned by the 2001 decision of the Privy Council in the Gairy case in Grenada. The Privy Council held in that case that the

Minister of Finance of Grenada was obliged to pay monies found due for the unlawful acquisition of Gairy's property. The Privy Council also held that, under our constitution, government officials can be subject to orders of mandamus to protect fundamental rights. Breach of an order of mandamus can lead to imprisonment of the official responsible for making the payment.

The CCJ has shown very clearly from its inception that it will be similarly strong in the face of malfeasance by governments and government ministers. The reticent governments feel caught between a rock and a hard place. They will eventually move but for now they prefer what a senior St. Kitts and Nevis lawyer, who frequently represented the Douglas government, said – "to take their chances with the white people."

The events of the 26 Month Election have re-ignited the debate in St. Kitts and Nevis and the region on the wisdom of moving from the Privy Council to the CCJ.

I have not the slightest doubt of the capacity of the judges of the CCJ to provide top quality justice and of the structural and actual independence of that court from the governments of the region. I doubt however that if formally tested in St. Kitts and Nevis that view would prevail and particularly not at this time.

The decisions of the three levels of our courts in the 2015 Boundaries case have reinforced the unfortunate but widely held perception that the regionally based courts are not as strong as the Privy Council in protecting the fundamental rights of the people. Many people believe that some of our regionally based judges will not be able to resist the subtle and not so subtle pressures which they know Caribbean prime ministers will put on them. The facts do not bear this out but perception and confidence often prevail over actuality. It is partly and sadly a lack of self-confidence in the people that facilitates that perception. But there is also an understandable lack of confidence in the leadership of the region and serious doubt as to the commitment of Caribbean leaders to the rule of law and to democracy.

The perception of which I speak was graphically described in an editorial in the *Jamaica Observer* newspaper shortly after the St. Kitts and Nevis election. The editor wrote:

> We have, in the past, leaned towards supporting the idea of the CCJ, based on our very solid commitment to regionalism. But given developments, such as that in St. Kitts and Nevis, we are increasingly worried about dispensing with the UK Privy Council at this point in time.

Until we are certain that we will have in place a legal superstructure that mirrors the confidence inspired by the Privy Council, untouchable by local politics, it would be foolhardy to make the CCJ our final appellate court.

Our wise ancestors used to say "tek sleep mark death". The inexplicable rush to jettison the Privy Council in favour of a Caribbean court which is, at best, still a work in progress, could unravel what legal gains we have made in the region. This clearly is a case in which we must make haste slowly.

As to the future, the move to the CCJ will eventually come for all the islands but that move has been severely set back by the events in St. Kitts and Nevis. In any event there is an immediate need for a constitutional and administrative law division of the Eastern Caribbean Supreme Court staffed by experienced judges and with the infrastructure to respond quickly on a regular basis to urgent applications. That will require additional funding from the governments. Providing such funding would be one way for the governments to allay the lack of trust of their people of their commitment to the rule of law. It would in my opinion also enhance the justice system if a pool of judges were to be established in the region. The pool should comprise senior attorneys-at law from across the region who are prepared to do short term stints on that division of the court. It is already common for the court to engage lawyers from private practice to do short term stints on the bench in the Eastern Caribbean. The creation of a pool of judges would be an advancement of that concept and enable the region to share expertise.

Also, there are serious constraints, including low salaries, in recruiting judges in the OECS. As we are a multi country jurisdiction we also suffer because the Eastern Caribbean Supreme Court has to rely on financing from the nine member countries and territories all of whom are not always as forthcoming as they should be. We need a review of Judges' terms and conditions. We need a similar funding arrangement to that of the Caribbean Court of Justice to allow the court to achieve full financial independence.

Term Limits and Other Changes to the Constitution

Albert Einstein said *You can't solve a problem with the same mindset that created it.* It will take a monumental change in the existing mindset to achieve a two-thirds majority in separate referenda in St. Kitts and in Nevis as is required to change some, but not all, of the provisions of the constitution affecting the governance of the country. I will address in this chapter the changes that I advocate. I begin with those which can be made by two thirds votes in the National Assembly without the need for referenda.

CHANGES NOT REQUIRING REFERENDA

Term Limits

We have seen first hand that the rule of law can be overcome by the rule of man if the people are not vigilant especially as St. Kitts and Nevis lacks many of the traditional features of a constitutional democracy to promote accountability of the executive. We have no Freedom of Information legislation, no Integrity in Public Life legislation, no Campaign Finance legislation, no legislation regulating government tendering or purchasing of goods and services, not even legislation requiring government to publish its policies. All of these defects can be cured by legislation. But even if these changes are achieved, term limits are also essential.

The Phillips Task Force addressed the subject of term limits on page 30 of its report. It said this:

> It was strongly represented to the Task Force that a limit of two successive terms (not necessarily ten years) should be set for Parliamentarians, both elected and appointed. The person could re-enter Parliament after an intermission of one term. The Task Force feels that this proposal should be given serious consideration in all its aspects.

My view is that a prime minister should not serve in that office for more than two terms in total. This is an important lesson from the 26 Month Election.

I will take a brief look at the history of term limits and their prevalence in today's world. The ancient Greeks had term limits in their system of governance 2,700 years ago. The Romans had them around the time of Christ as do a large number of modern democracies. Two thirds of sub-Saharan African countries have them. Almost all of Latin America does as well and a large number of Asian countries have them. They are not however common in Europe or in the Commonwealth Caribbean. The United States restricts its President to two terms but does not limit terms of Representatives and Senators in its Congress.

Let's look at the arguments for and against term limits.

- The main argument against them is that voters are deprived of their right to elect whomsoever they want to public office.

- It is also argued that removing longer serving politicians from office can result in the election of inexperienced politicians.

- Another argument is that when an elected politician is coming to the end of his term and cannot seek re-election he does not have to heed the concerns of his constituents and can use his power to set himself up in the future whereas if he had to face the electorate he would have to worry about how voters think.

- It is also argued that you do not necessarily get better leaders by rotating them.

The main arguments in favour of term limits are:
- they prevent persons in power from using that power to remain in office indefinitely;

- they make room for fresh candidates, new faces, and encourage participation in the process;

- they deter politicians from making choices solely to prolong their career; and

- they recognize the negative impact which power can have on human nature.

I used to think, when I was young and idealistic, that term limits were not necessary because no one would want to subject himself for too long to the pressures of political power. It is interesting that the framers of the US constitution seem to have held that view because the term limitation on the US President was imposed only in 1951. But after 50 years of watching our democracy, I have changed my mind principally on the basis of the last argument that I recited in favour of term limits that is, they recognize the negative impact which power can have on human nature. While the world has in terms of its physical conditions advanced in the 2700 years since the Greeks imposed term limits, human nature has remained the same.

Term limits are rare in Commonwealth countries because we inherited the British system which does not have that feature as part of its political system. The issue is however being hotly debated in our region, particularly among our youth. It featured in the debate in St. Vincent on constitutional reform which, for other reasons, failed in a referendum. In 2014 term limits were imposed in Trinidad and Tobago and they are under consideration in the constitutional reform process in Grenada.

In considering this issue we should look at the pecularities of our system. As I said we do not have a true separation of powers. We have an elective dictatorship and an office of Prime Minister which can, as has been very apparent, be easily used by any holder to manipulate almost everything and everybody. And we have a political tribalism that promotes hatred and the one-sided exercise of political power, that aggrandizes and almost deifies politicians and demonises others. We have an entitlements mentality which says that government must provide for all our desires, the result of which is that, given its financial limitations, government cannot satisfy everyone's needs and therefore favours some over others. We have a country motto of 'Country above Self' but in practice it is 'Party above all else'. This form of politics, which none of our leaders of the past has tried to change, makes it extremely difficult for a leader to provide balanced governance for a long period of time, no matter how idealistic he or she may have been when he or she began in politics. It encourages instead an autocratic and self-centered application of power which degrades the objectivity of a politician who is in it for too long.

In my opinion there should be a limit of four terms (a maximum of 20 years) for elected representatives in the National Assembly; subject to that limitation, a limit of two terms (a maximum of 10 years) for Prime Minister; and two terms (a maximum of 10 years) for non-elected Senators.

Maximum Time for Tabling Motion of No Confidence

Another change which does not require approval by referenda is the addition to the constitution of a fixed time within which a Motion of No Confidence must be brought before the National Assembly for debate and a vote. This should go without saying but its inclusion would avoid on that ground a repeat of the 26 Month Election. No more than 14 days should be allowed from filing to the sitting of the Assembly to debate the Motion.

There should also be an amendment expressly to enable the Court to mandate a Speaker to comply with the requirement.

Political parties are not officially recognised in our constitution. This is because we have a constituency system under which each constituency elects as its representative a person who is qualified (in accordance with the constitution and any laws made under it) to sit as a member in the National Assembly. Membership of or allegiance to a political party is not a qualifying requirement in the constitution or any law made under it. Nor do the provisions relating to voting in the Assembly say anything about political parties.

The provisions of section 52(2) for appointment of a Prime Minister also reflect the independence of Representatives (in that capacity) by providing that *whenever the Governor General has occasion to appoint a Prime Minister he shall appoint a Representative who appears to him likely to command the support of the majority of the Representatives*. No mention whatever is made of political parties nor is there any other constraint on how the Representative determines whom he supports. It is the same with section 52(6) dealing with removal of the prime minister following a vote of no confidence. Those sections leave it open to Representatives to give their support to any other Representative after a general election and to vote as he or she wishes on a vote of no confidence. It is on this basis that coalitions are formed to assume executive power and prime ministers are removed by vote of no confidence. If the leader of a political party whose members hold the majority of seats in the Assembly was automatically entitled to be prime minister for a full term of five years there would be no need for the discretion given to the Governor General in section 52(2) nor for the provisions for a vote of no confidence in section 52(6).

The vote of 'no confidence' is the counter balance created by the constitution to the overwhelming powers given to the prime minister.

Those powers are vested personally in the man or woman who holds the office and not in him or her as leader of a political party. The prime minister is not bound to follow any party positions and can bring any member of the Assembly (regardless of party affiliation) into the cabinet. This balancing power or safeguard is also the major instance of the separation of powers between the legislative and executive branches of government. The prime minister controls appointments to the Executive by virtue of section 52(4) of the constitution. That section provides that *"appointments to the office of Minister, other than the office of Prime Minister, shall be made by the Governor-General acting in accordance with the advice of the Prime Minister, from among members of the National Assembly".* Section 52(9)(a) provides *that "the office of a Minister other than the Prime Minister shall become vacant if the Governor General, acting in accordance with the advice of the Prime Minister, so directs."* In essence the prime minister appoints and removes cabinet members. Likewise the Representatives can in effect appoint or remove him.

While a cabinet member is a part of the executive and legislative branches of government, those roles are still separate and membership of the cabinet does not bind a Representative to vote in any particular way in the National Assembly. A Representative may expose himself to removal from the Executive (Cabinet) if he votes in the Assembly in a manner dissatisfactory to the prime minister (and may risk re-election) but that is his right as a member of the legislative branch of government representing his constituency.

The 26 Month Election showed in practice how all of the above provisions work or, in the case of the Motion of No Confidence, should work.

Fiscal Responsibility

The constitution should also be amended to enforce fiscal responsibility. There should be two amendments to this end, the first setting a maximum of government debt at a fixed percentage of GDP and the second requiring balanced budgets. Exceptions should be allowed only with support of the public determined by ballot at a General Election or in a referendum or, in cases of genuine emergency, a two thirds vote in the Assembly. This country almost fell off the cliff in debt and was saved only by the timidity of its creditors in accepting the loss of a major part of their rights, known as 'taking a haircut'. A country will not get away many times with that type of shenanigan and should not boast about it as happened here.

The amendment should impose direct personal liability on any government minister or official who participates in the infringement of the fiscal limitations.

Issue Ballots

A system should be established to permit specific issues to be put to the people at an election or separate referendum. Changes to the fiscal responsibility provisions referred to in the above section could be determined in this way.

Election of Speaker

The 26 Month Election showed the need for the Speaker of the House of Assembly to be elected by ballot rather than by the governing party. Rather than being appointed by the National Assembly, the Speaker should be elected by the electorate in a ballot at the time of each general election. While that would not guarantee his independence, it would expose candidates to public scrutiny.

Removal of Bryant Clause

Section 27 of the constitution provides that to be qualified for election to or appointment as Senator of the National Assembly, a person must be a citizen of St Kitts and Nevis, of the age of 21 and upwards, and have one parent born in St Kitts and Nevis, and be domiciled there at the date of his nomination. This section is referred to as the 'Bryant clause' because its effect (many think intention) was to prevent Fitzroy Bryant, who had served as a minister of government under Labour administrations pre-independence, to qualify post-independence to become a candidate for election. Bryant who was born in Antigua, had become a citizen by residence under the Statehood constitution and his citizenship continued after independence. However, after independence, section 27 deprived him of the right to contest an election for the National Assembly as neither he nor his parents were born in St. Kitts. Section 27 has no place in a modern constitution. Qualification for election should not be based only on citizenship. People who buy citizenship should be excluded in any event. The constitution should allow qualification based on citizenship by birth, descent or long term residence. As the constitution stands, residence is not a requirement for election. Thus we have the anomaly that a citizen who was born abroad and has never lived here but who has a parent born here can qualify but not a person like Bryant, born in Antigua but who spent most of his life here.

Removal of Dual Nationality Clause

Section 28 of the constitution is referred to as the 'dual nationality clause'. It provides that a person is NOT qualified to be elected to or appointed as a Senator of the National Assembly, if by virtue of his own act, he is under any acknowledgment of allegiance, obedience or adherence to a foreign power or state. That clause creates the ridiculous anomaly that a person who was born in St. Kitts and Nevis and then takes a second nationality of choice cannot seek elective office or become a senator , but his son or daughter who was born abroad and has two nationalities, may not be debarred.

Strengthening the Right of Free Speech

The fundamental right of free speech should be strengthened by the addition of provisions that allow the public to exercise that right effectively in relation to government-owned media. The courts have ruled in recent years that candidates for political office have a fundamental right of access to the government - owned media. That was agreed by all political parties as long ago as 1994 in the 'Four Seasons Accord', but to no avail. Provisions should be added to the constitution to guarantee that access to the public and to allow for independent monitoring of the use of government media. Access to government-owned media is part of our fundamental right of free speech and should be fully and meaningfully implemented. That is another lesson of the 26 Month Election. The charade that took place on election night on *ZIZ TV* should not be allowed to happen again.

Election of Ombudsman

The Ombudsman should also be an elected position under the constitution. That would give the holder of that office greater independence and powers to protect the citizen from the abuse of government power. It would also give the office higher profile. Very little is heard of the Ombudsman or his work under the current legislation. If he were removed from the influence of the prime minister the office might be more effective to protect the interests of the citizen in his or her dealings with the public service.

CHANGES REQUIRING REFERENDA

Constituency System

There is a strong argument for the replacement of the constituency system with a system of proportional representation or a combination of both. There are grounds too for more localized government e.g local councils with limited powers. There are models in the Caribbean and all over the world which can be studied for application or adaptation. This is an excellent topic for research and debate in the CFB College and in the High Schools to sensitise our people, particularly the young who may have to decide. Civil society should also initiate this discussion outside of the political process and elements.

I support the view expressed as follows by the late Professor Simeon MacIntosh, who was Dean of the Faculty of Law at UWI and Professor Emeritus of Law at Howard University in Washington, U.S.A.

> In light of the foregoing discussion and having regard to our history, political culture and economic circumstances, we can make an informed choice as to whether or not we should retain the current electoral model or adopt some form of proportional representation. It is an undisputed fact that one of the worst dangers to democratic governance in the Commonwealth Caribbean is the potential for abuse of power by the 'elective dictatorship' of prime ministerial government. The 'winner-take-all' situation or 'to the victor the spoils' mentality that our current electoral system indulges compounds the problem ten-fold. As Professor Selwyn Ryan observes, our Westminster-type democracy, under a 'winner-take-all' electoral rule, has encouraged a too destructive competition for political office. It has placed too heavy a concentration of power in the hands of the ruling elites, and has encouraged the marginalization and alienation of a substantial part of the population from participation in the governance and development of their society. On this view, it would seem that proportional representation is the more attractive electoral system. (*Caribbean Constitutional Reform: Rethinking the West Indian Polity.* 2002, Kingston, The Caribbean Law Publishing Company)

I agree entirely with these views. The constituency system adds to our culture of political patronage, which like the political tribalism from which we suffer, is a yoke on our country's democracy and we are a very small country – in fact we are really a village in international terms. We do not need a constituency representative to lean on to improve conditions in our constituencies. Any government Minister is just as reachable as any constituency representative.

Proportional representation would change for the better our system of political campaigning. It would help to shift the focus from personalities to issues. The inclination to deify a party's candidate and demonise his opponent would be lessened. While the competence of individual politicians will always be relevant to elections, the removal of multiple head to head election races will help to focus the election debate on issues.

The Role of Senators

The role of senators in the Assembly was also highlighted by the 26 Month Election and should be reviewed. In a small Parliament like ours the vote of senators can carry great weight. The votes of senators were influential in the passage of the Senators Bill which was later struck down by the court. If the Act was allowed to stand there could have been a total of 7 senators which is far too many with only 11 elected Representatives.

Based on the recent experience, it is argued that the constitution should be changed to prevent senators from voting on legislation to expand their number. There is ground also to require that the Assembly should debate the nominees for senator before they are appointed. While that would not guarantee that competent people would be appointed it would allow scrutiny in public of such nominees. The reduction in political partisanship would help in the appointment of persons to the office of senator who will exercise mature and independent judgment and not just be puppets, but the constitutional provisions should be revisited.

Electoral System

The 26 Month Election showed beyond the shadow of a doubt that a completely new electoral system is required. While this can be achieved for the most part by legislation many of the provisions should be made part of the constitution. These are addressed in the next chapter.

8. *The Electoral System*

Free and fair elections are essential ingredients of a true democracy. The word free connotes that persons who are entitled to register as voters and to vote in elections are not unreasonably impeded (by fear or compulsion or otherwise) in their exercise of those rights in accordance with applicable laws. Fairness is a more elusive concept but is generally accepted to connote that there are laws that reasonably provide for the conduct of elections, that there are genuinely equal opportunities for all competing candidates, that the electoral process is under control independent of the politicians and that there are transparent regulations as to how persons are registered to vote.

In a small country like St. Kitts and Nevis, with a constituency and 'winner take all' system and approximately 30,000 registered voters, a few votes can make the difference in deciding which political party forms the government in an election. The slightest abuse or distortion of or error in the system can therefore have a significant effect. By and large elections in St. Kitts and Nevis have been free but not fair. I will point out some of the reasons for the lack of fairness and make suggestions for improvements.

THE OVERSEAS VOTE

It is important to note that the right to vote is not a fundamental right given by the constitution to all citizens but one that can be circumscribed by legislation. It is incorrect therefore, to assume that citizens resident overseas have an automatic right to vote. A large number of countries tie the right to vote to residence in the country. The United States is one country which does not but, it is important to note, the United States makes all citizens wherever resident pay income tax on their worldwide income. Those who inherit from them are also liable to death duties on the deceased citizen's assets worldwide. To that extent US citizens wherever they reside pay for their government and have a direct interest in the election of their government. The US has a population of three hundred million and an electorate of over one hundred million people. A few thousand overseas votes do not have the same impact in the US as a few dozen votes here which can decide an election. Citizens of St. Kitts and Nevis who reside abroad do not have to pay income taxes here. While I agree that some pay property taxes and many bank their money here or send remittances that number is small compared to the tens of thousands who have no vested interest whatever in the country but are eligible to register to vote in elections here. Many do not put foot here except to register and to vote.

In this regard I quote from the late Sir Lee Moore, former Premier of St. Kitts-Nevis and a revered member of the Labour party, as reported in the edition of *The Labour Spokesman* newspaper of November 2, 1983:

> the people living in St. Kitts and Nevis could find their wishes overruled by people living abroad"...[this can...] " subvert democracy, making the exercise of the franchise of no effect and giving rise to instability in the country."

Moore said also that there are

> "differences between citizenship and the franchise, citizenship being concerned with allegiance and protection, the franchise being related to place of residence.

The same Labour party blamed its defeat in the 2015 election on the late arrival of two of its 20-plus charter flights. Its leader gave the exact numbers of persons who were on those flights intended to vote in two named constituencies. That was a blatant admission that it was relying on the overseas vote. It is an abomination that plane-loads of citizens can fly in just before, vote on election day and fly out the same or next day. At least 10 per cent of the voters in the 2015 General Election were overseas voters.

I recall the true story of a well-dressed lady who was asked at the ferry terminal in Basseterre on an election day where she was coming from. She said in her American accent that she was coming from Nevis where she had just voted. She continued *"I did not know Nevis was so nice."* Can we really have fair elections when plane charters can decide the result?

How did we get there? The first election under adult suffrage took place under the Constitution and Elections Ordinance 1952. Under that law residence was an absolute requirement for registration as a voter. It remained in effect until November 8, 1983, less than two months after

Independence Day, when it was changed by the National Assembly with the PAM/NRP majority. The amending law gave the right to register to vote to a citizen of St. Kitts and Nevis of the age of eighteen years or upwards if resident or domiciled in the country at the date of registration. Residence was removed as an absolute requirement for a citizen to vote. *Domicil* is a nebulous legal concept and should not be used as a criterion for voting. To qualify as domiciled in the country all a citizen resident abroad has to say is that one day he or she intends to come to St. Kitts or Nevis to live. That question is not even asked of those who register. No rules were put in place to determine to which constituency an overseas voter belonged for registration purposes. It meant that a citizen could essentially choose where he would register. You do not have to be a rocket scientist to realize that overseas voters could be registered to suit the interests of the party which they support. And that is exactly what happened. And, not surprisingly, the practice developed of moving resident citizens around to suit the interests of the party they support.

I asked a senior member of the PAM party long after that party had lost power in 1995 why they decided on so lax a law. He said that they did not intend the free for all that has resulted but that, under the old system, some of their members, who had moved to the Virgin Islands and wanted to come home to vote, had been knocked off the voters list on objections from Labour representatives. I said to him cynically in reply that they had opened a Pandora's box which they no longer had the opportunity to close. They did not have the opportunity at the time of my conversation but the new government has it after the 26 Month Election. The overseas vote should be eliminated and the right to vote should be based only on residence. The exact period should be open for debate.

ELECTORAL REFORM

The Labour party won the 1995 elections and those of 2000 and 2004. In 2006 the Labour government initiated a reform process which, it said, resulted from the review of the report of the Commonwealth Expert Team of the 2004 elections, the report of the Caricom Observers of the 2004 election and the report of the Commonwealth Assessment Mission of 2005. The government said that the review would implement the commitment given by the Labour party in its 2000 manifesto *to overhaul the voters list to eliminate any perception of fraud.*

A very elaborate process was designed including the establishment of five committees, one being the Electoral Reform Consultative Committee as part of a process that was intended to be concluded by 2007. The Reform Committee (as I will call it) consulted with the public and with civil society groups. The PAM party, the creators of the mess, refused to participate. The Reform Committee issued a report which recommended a complete re-registration of voters. Given the very strong and widely held perception (many would say knowledge) of fraud in the existing list and the recommendation of the Reform Committee for a complete re-registration of voters it was generally expected that the law would provide for a new voters list as had been the case recently in Antigua.

A Commonwealth Assessment Mission recommended likewise. The Mission comprised two regional experts, one of whom was the late David Thompson then Leader of the Opposition and later Prime Minister of Barbados . Thompson was a good friend of the Labour party. The Mission said this in its report:

> The current voters list is based on an archaic system that is inadequate to provide the necessary tools for the efficient, transparent and effective management of the registration of voters, the checking of duplicates, the production of lists and the production of ID cards.

> The Mission believes that the acquisition of a modern system will go a long way toward addressing the issues above and we suggest that the proposed new Electoral and Boundaries Commission conducts a new enumeration exercise where the old list is discarded and new registration exercise commenced with clearer laws and regulations addressing residency and registration to provide a clean voters list that is a result of a partnership between the institutions charged with the responsibility and the major stakeholders in electoral matters.

The use by the Mission of the word 'clean' suggests to me that it accepted that the current list was unclean. However, instead of starting afresh as had been recommended, the old deficient legislation was only amended in part. The National Assembly Elections (Amendment) Act 2007 introduced a politically contrived process called 'reconstruction ' of the old list under which a voter on the old list could 'confirm' his registration by a fixed time if not he could be struck off the list on reconstruction. On confirmation, the voter would receive one of the new ID cards. Persons eligible to vote who did not confirm their registration or who had not previously registered could register in compliance with the new provisions for resident and overseas voters.

As noted, the amending Act retained the overseas vote. The amendments did not establish the transparency so badly needed to determine the constituency in which a voter would be registered nor did it provide a workable and fair dispute resolution process to deal with objections.

To compound matters, the new law maintained the unfair and ridiculous requirement that a person objecting to registration of a voter based on his place of residence had to prove that the voter does not live where he says he does. Most countries require the voter to prove his residence by documentary evidence – utility bills, social security registration, passport or driver's licence. The Chamber of Commerce presented to the Reform Committee a detailed form which it proposed be completed by each applicant to be registered to verify his residence under sanction of perjury. The Chamber suggested adoption of the system used in Trinidad and Tobago where registration officers verify residence by visits to the address given by the applicant. That would be very workable in a small country. The Chamber presentation is still very relevant and is attached in its entirety in an Appendix.

None of these recommendations was accepted. Instead the earlier fraud was entrenched and it became just as easy for new fraud to be perpetrated. The result is that we have a system which is better only in having voter ID cards and in having removed the names of dead persons from the voters list. Thus we continue to have free but not fair elections.

I quote again from the Report of the 2005 Commonwealth Assessment Mission:

> The Mission was inundated with complaints about the possibility of party supporters from stronghold constituencies to register in marginal ones in order to boost the party's chances of winning seats. If true this practice would make a mockery of the present constituency system, which is the basis for the First-Past the-Post electoral system, which obtains in St. Kitts and Nevis.

That mockery remains as another reason for our 'brooding democracy'.

CAMPAIGN FINANCE LEGISLATION

Another change which I advocate is the introduction of campaign finance laws to avoid elections being bought. Election campaigns have become an expensive process and while it is important to our democracy that those seeking office get their message out and that costs money, there comes a point at which money can undermine the system. Elections should not be bought. Those who provide vast sums expect a return on their investment and that return is usually provided not by those who received the money, but by the country. I cannot put the argument any better than did Anthony Carmona, the President of Trinidad and Tobago in an address to Parliament on August 2, 2013, when he declared that *'Election campaign financing is a veritable juggernaut that results in financiers arrogating political power unto themselves and thereby undermining the system of governance'.*

And that *'The time has come when we must bite the bullet of campaign financing reform and introduce appropriate transparency and accountability in the management of the country's electoral system'.* We here in St Kitts and Nevis should take that advice.

The need for campaign finance laws is even greater here because of the overseas vote. I have never heard an advertisement stating what the cost is of a ticket for that purpose from London, New York or Toronto. Some legal minds are of the view that it constitutes electoral bribery to provide a charter for overseas voters, but whether that is good legal opinion or not, the public has the right to know who provides the money for the charters and the other massive spending on election campaigns. Even if the overseas vote is eliminated, that right to know should, in my opinion be recognised as a fundamental right in the constitution, which should also set out the structure of the system of disclosure. That would set the framework for the necessary legislation and make it more difficult to frustrate the right.

Campaign finance legislation is essential also to avoid aspersions being cast against politicians who receive large donations for themselves or their party that they are in the pocket of political donors. Such legislation was one of the recommendations made in the May 2005 report of the Advisory Committee on remuneration for members of the Federal Parliament in St. Kitts and Nevis. The government of the day readily accepted the pay increases for parliamentarians and ministers of government recommended in the report but ignored the recommendation for campaign finance legislation. Salaries of parliamentarians and ministers are still relatively modest. It is important for democracy that the citizenry can feel confident that their representatives are not on the take to augment their salaries. Corruption usually starts from the top and where it is perceived rightly or wrongly to exist it spreads like wild fire throughout the public service. There are examples of this all over the world.

I set out one of the comments of the Advisory Committee on this subject:

> We fully endorse this expressed need [in the Venner Report quoted above] for priority attention to be afforded to some meaningful statutory regulation of electoral financing, and recommend accordingly. Left unaddressed, this has serious potential to undermine the democratic gains made in Caribbean societies. There is ample scope for St. Kitts and Nevis to become a leader in the region in this regard. To fail to address this issue in a timely manner is to run the real risk of the Caribbean being perceived by our own people and others further afield as a region in which public life can be degraded by unscrupulous practices. We recommend that specific legislation with concrete and effective measures be put in place urgently to guard against this risk. Our history demands not only that our leaders not be bought or sold, but that we proudly proclaim that this is virtually impossible and that any attempts to do so would be subject to criminal sanctions imposed by law.

SUPERVISOR OF ELECTIONS

The public officer responsible for the day to day operations of the electoral process is the Supervisor of Elections whose responsibility is given by the constitution as *to exercise general supervision over the registration of voters in elections of Representatives and over the conduct of such elections.* The Supervisor of Elections is appointed by the Governor-General acting in his own deliberate judgment after consulting the Prime Minister and the Leader of the Opposition. This appointment is one of the few instances where the Governor General is given power by the constitution to act in his own deliberate judgment. Another such instance is the appointment of the Chairman of the Electoral Commission. The Governor General therefore plays a key role in the sanctity of the electoral process.

Leroy Benjamin, Supervisor of Elections before the infamous Wingrove George was forced to resign the position in 2012 after the High Court found and the Court of Appeal confirmed that he had misconducted a by-election in Nevis. Then George was appointed. There is no need to repeat his misconduct.

There has been much debate over the years on the role of the Governor General. Suffice it to say at this point that if we can't trust the Governor General's exercise of this power then we are in a bad way and I am reminded of the statement by Sir Fred Phillips in his book *Commonwealth Caribbean Constitutional Law:* (2002, London, Cavendish)

> We hope in the preceding pages we have shown that a Constitution is not an end in itself, it is how a constitutional instrument is permitted to work that matters. The most well intentioned instrument may easily become entirely counter- productive.

In other language, the way the men charged with responsibility act is as important as the words of the constitution. A constitution becomes entirely counter-productive when persons expected to act independently fail to do so.

One way of facilitating the Supervisor of Elections in acting independently is to extricate him or her from any direct reliance on the prime minister or cabinet for administrative or financial support. The entire electoral system should be given an ample annual budget voted by the National Assembly on advice from the Electoral Commission. Appointment of every officer in the electoral office should be made, on application, by the Supervisor with the approval of the Electoral Commission. The administrative structure of the Electoral Office and the names, qualifications and duties of every such officer should be published in the local newspapers. The names of every applicant for any electoral position should be published in advance of appointment to allow representations to be made to the Supervisor and the Commission as to the suitability and independence of the applicant. That would not entirely prevent abuse of the system but it would subject it to greater public scrutiny.

THE ELECTORAL COMMISSION

In a passage from the report of the Commonwealth Assessment team quoted earlier in this chapter, the report refers to 'the proposed new Electoral and Boundaries Commission'. They recommend the expansion of the Commission which they noted did not at the time include a nominee of the opposition party in St. Kitts. That is because the Electoral Commission comprises only three persons one nominated by the Prime Minister, one by the Leader of the Opposition and the Chairman appointed by the Governor General acting in his own deliberate judgment. The Chairman must be a legal practitioner with at least seven years of practice of the law.

The function of the Electoral Commission is ' to supervise the Supervisor of Elections in the exercise of his function*s*....' For the Commission to carry outs its functions more effectively we need a larger Electoral Commission with stronger provisions to ensure its independence from political interference. The budget provided for the electoral system should include adequate funding to enable the Commission to have its own secretariat and its own office and to take independent legal and other advice. The Commission should be required by the Constitution to issue a full and complete report after each election. The electorate should not have to rely solely on reports from outside observers.

The Commonwealth Assessment Team proposed a joint Electoral and Boundaries Commission. At present there is a separate Boundaries Commission which is a purely political body and, as the 26 Month Election has shown, a recipe for gerrymandering. If we were to move to a system of proportional representation there would be no need for a Boundaries Commission. If we retain the current system then I agree with the Commonwealth Assessment Team that there should be a joint Electoral and Boundaries Commission with the political element removed.

DISPUTE RESOLUTION AS TO VOTER REGISTRATION

It is a grave deficiency to give registration officers the power to resolve disputes involving voter registration. This process is a legal one which requires due process including the taking of evidence from and cross examination of witnesses, the careful consideration of arguments as to the facts and writing decisions. Even if there were a transparent process for the appointment of registration officers it is not a power which should be exercised by them. That process should be assigned to legally trained officials, either a magistrate or high court judge. The legislation should mandate the expeditious hearing of disputes of this type and require the government to provide all resources required for the purpose.

COMMONWEALTH CITIZENS

The constitution provides for citizens of Commonwealth countries to vote in elections here subject to conditions established by legislation.

The legislative provisions have since independence set a residential requirement of a minimum of one year. Many Commonwealth countries allow nationals of other Commonwealth countries this right but the residential requirement varies. In Antigua for example the residential requirement was three years and has recently been increased to seven. In a small country where margins of victory are often small, one year is in my opinion too short a period for a Commonwealth citizen to establish a connection with the country that gives him or her a real stake in its governance.

The current system has been abused to high heaven. One such abuse is in the registration of students of offshore universities. Such students are by definition transitory and have absolutely no stake in the country other than attending the university for the degree period. It is preposterous, if at all it is legal, for this to continue.

There is a growing community of Commonwealth citizens residing in St Kitts and Nevis. I welcome law abiding Commonwealth citizens who can contribute to our economy without marginalising the local citizens. However they should not be able to swing an election with their votes which is now a real possibility. A businessman of Indian origin boasted to me that he controls 400 votes in East Basseterre of Indian nationals resident there. An exaggeration perhaps, but the margin of victory in that seat was four votes.

The minimum residential requirement should be seven years to coincide with the period after which a resident of a Commonwealth country can obtain permanent residence.

Accountable and
9. Transparent Governance
and Public Boards

emocracy is not an election every five years but an everyday process. It requires open and accountable governance and that the people be properly informed on what the government is doing in their name. It requires that the people be conscious of their rights and of the obligations of those whom they elect; that they speak out against abuses of power and against secretive behaviour of their leaders; democracy should never be taken for granted.

Associated Statehood was established in 1967 under a constitution that gave very substantial control over the internal affairs of the State to the executive headed by the Premier. Save for the protection of fundamental rights, that constitution contained very limited checks and balances on the exercise of that power. It provided a basic system for financial management of the State by way of a Consolidated Fund, budgetary provisions and oversight by the Director of Audit. There was no provision however for ongoing disclosure by the executive in the exercise of its powers of financial management and no provision for regulating the procurement by government of goods and services. The constitution provided a framework for appointments to the public service but again this was very basic. The 1983 Independence Constitution contained similar provisions and no greater obligations on the part of the executive (prime minister and cabinet) for accountability and transparency.

My recollection of the process of public debate leading to independence is that the emphasis was on the relationship between St. Kitts and Nevis and on the fundamental rights provisions. Governance issues were not prominent in the debate. That, with the benefit of hindsight, was a terrible error. Accountable and transparent government are essential ingredients of a true democracy. The statehood and independence arrangements ignored this fact. There were too many assumptions, including an assumption of integrity on the part of those who would govern and an assumption of adherence to

British conventions. The short history of independent St. Kitts and Nevis, and most vividly the 26 Month Election, has shown that if something is not written in a law, the country should not expect its leaders to honour it. That is sad but true.

If it was assumed that the government would, after independence, legislate adequate checks and balances on itself that too was a naïve assumption. It has not happened in the three decades since independence. Instead the powers of the executive have been augmented by politicisation of the public service and virtually unaccountable control of government assets and of the procurement process.

A conference on the Quality of Life in St. Kitts and Nevis after 25 years of Self Government was organised by several civil society bodies and held from June 12–14, 1992. The overriding lament at the conference was the excessive political polarisation of the country. The state of governance was also addressed. In a presentation to the conference on moral values and attitudes, Sir Probyn Inniss, a former Governor during Statehood and a distinguished lawyer and historian, declared:

> It is interesting to note that many of the controls which were exercised by the colonial masters - and which local political leaders complained about bitterly, when they did not control the levers of power – (those controls) remain as firmly in place today as they did 25 years ago.
>
> Independence has brought about a transfer of power from Downing Street (or wherever) to Church Street [Basseterre, St. Kitts]. But has anything really changed?
>
> Compared to 25 years ago, an immense amount of power is concentrated in the hands of whoever heads the Government of the day. Compared to 25 years ago, there is no plantocracy to challenge what it perceives to be abuse of power by the Government. No plantocracy to provide a safe haven for those who for one reason or another cannot find employment with the Government. It is estimated that Government controls directly and indirectly about 70% of the jobs in St. Kitts-Nevis. It controls the National Radio and Television System.
>
> On the other hand one of the great legacies of the colonial era – a Neutral and Impartial Civil Service ~ has been virtually destroyed. The only remaining bastion is the Judiciary.

Every country that espouses democracy should keep under constant review its governance standards and legislation. That review process is even more essential in young democracies and small countries such as St. Kitts and Nevis. The inadequacy of our constitution adds to that need.

You could not find a more poignant but realistic description of the problem than in this paragraph from the inauguration address of President Carmona of Trinidad and Tobago in 2013:

> For many, many years the ship called the Republic of Trinidad and Tobago has left its safe moorings of integrity, accountability, responsibility, transparency and inclusiveness. We are good at sound bites and labeling. We can be excellent wordsmiths. The cynics, they howl in the wilderness. But if we are to establish a better, more progressive, more humane society, real change must be invoked.

And so (in relation to this country) say many of the persons in St. Kitts and Nevis who think objectively.

Three decades after independence, St. Kitts and Nevis still operates in effect under the colonial era General Orders. Lip service has been paid to modernisation of the civil service but that has not happened for obvious reasons. The General Orders focused power in one man, the British Administrator. Those powers are now in practice exercised by the prime minister.

There are many very competent and responsible civil servants who approach their work in a professional manner. Some government departments provide good public service but there are too many civil servants who think they are untouchable and need not be productive. There is nothing civil about some government departments. You go there to beg for a favour or so they see it. The system has been politicized and manipulated to promote partisanship and that severely limits the impact of the true professionals in the service.

The attitudes and patronage that prevail do not only militate against good governance but they negatively impact efficiency and productivity and hence economic development. They promote corruption, affect social cohesion, and undermine the rule of law.

How then can government be made more open and accountable and efficient? In my view efficiency should be part of this debate because public sector efficiency is critical to economic development and inefficiency undermines good governance.

Laws are required to create the transparency and accountability that our constitutional situation deters. However laws alone will not achieve that goal. There must be a change of attitude towards governance on the part of politicians. They must change the literal implementation of the 'winner take all' principle and the patronage which follows.

No single legislative measure will produce transparency and good governance. But a combination of the right measures can help if properly respected by those who govern and if properly enforced. In small countries with limited resources and a limited number of independent people to administer legislation, the enforcement processes must of necessity be simple. The aim should be as much to deter misconduct as to punish offenders. Public awareness and public pressure are as important as legislation in deterring misconduct. Civil society therefore plays a key role in ensuring the introduction into law of measures to promote transparency and good governance and the effectiveness of those measures.

I will comment on some appropriate measures.

INTEGRITY IN PUBLIC LIFE

After more than 20 years of public debate the last St. Kitts and Nevis government, seeking to score political points in the face of the Motion of No Confidence and having frustrated a Bill on the subject tabled by Opposition members, introduced the *Integrity in Public Life Act* which was enacted in August 2013. However, the Act requires a Ministerial Order to bring it into force and, not surprisingly, that was not forthcoming in the life of that government.

The 2013 Integrity in Public Life Act is inadequate and should be ditched and replaced by legislation which creates, to as great an extent as is possible, isolation of the regulatory body and process from political interference. To give, as the Act does, the prime minister and the leader of the opposition a major say in appointment of the personnel to whom they will report their assets is the clearest conflict of interest.

I suggest a role under the Act for the Director of Audit, with enhanced powers and resources. This is an area in which the OECS can give true effect to their proposed economic union by establishing a sub-regional Integrity Commission. As happens with the court system and regulation of the banking and securities systems, regionalisation will in some measure detach the integrity system from local influences.

In short, there should be two levels of reporting, the first to the Director of Audit with oversight by an OECS Integrity Commission. The Commission should also have the power to enforce the code of political conduct just as the Eastern Caribbean Central Bank has power of oversight of banks and the Eastern Caribbean Securities Regulatory Commission has oversight of the securities market.

One good aspect of the legislation (standing in limbo) is that it establishes a code of political conduct. The OECS should establish a common code of political conduct just as there is a banking code and a securities code. That should lessen the need for prime ministers of OECS countries to have to scold any of their colleagues on the day after an election as happened on February 17, 2015.

FREEDOM OF INFORMATION

The constitution of St. Kitts and Nevis proclaims several fundamental rights to protect democracy. These include freedom of thought, freedom of expression, including freedom to hold opinions without interference, freedom to receive ideas and information without interference and freedom to communicate ideas and opinions without interference. The constitution provides for the court to protect those rights.

To give effect to the fundamental right to information many democracies enact legislation often known as the 'Freedom of Information' or 'Access to Information Act'. The purpose of such legislation is best described in the Access to Information Act of Jamaica as:

> The objects of this Act are to reinforce and give further effect to certain fundamental principles underlying the system of constitutional democracy, namely–
>
> (a) governmental accountability;
>
> (b) transparency; and
>
> (c) public participation in national decision-making,
>
> by granting to the public a general right of access to official documents held by public authorities, subject to exemptions which balance that right against the public interest in exempting from disclosure governmental, commercial or personal information of a sensitive nature.

This type of legislation creates a balancing act between the right of the citizen to know and the obvious public interest in keeping some information confidential. It requires public authorities (usually including government ministries, departments and agencies, government authorities and boards, statutory corporations and government controlled companies) to make available on request by a member of the public certain information relating to the functions, decisions, policies and operations of the public authority. The secret information and documents exempted from disclosure include (with some qualifications) cabinet papers; information the disclosure of which would prejudice the security, defence or international relations of the country; confidential communications with foreign governments and international organizations; documents and information relating to law enforcement; information and documents subject to parliamentary privilege or legal professional privilege; information and documents the disclosure of which could have a substantial adverse effect on the economy; documents containing trade secrets, information of commercial value or sensitivity; and information and documents relating to the personal affairs of any person.

Sometimes the exemption lasts for a limited period. That period is 20 years in Jamaica.

The Governor General, the courts, the security and intelligence services and other public authorities so designated by Parliament are totally exempted from the Jamaica legislation.

Legislation of this type usually establishes the process available to the citizen for application for disclosure of information and the timelines and process for response by the public authority. If the public authority considers it proper to decline to disclose the requested information there is a process for notification of the decision and appeal by the citizen against it. Legislation usually contains oversight mechanisms to enforce the right. Some legislation provides for an official by various names e.g. an Information Commissioner. Such official carries out the oversight role. Various powers and protections are given to such an official to give effect to his role and to protect his independence.

Freedom of Information legislation often also requires public bodies to publish information about their functions and operations, their policies and processes.

Some provide protection for whistleblowers.

In 2013 an 'economic citizen' showed up at a Canadian airport with a St. Kitts and Nevis diplomatic passport and claimed the purpose of his visit was to meet with the Canadian Prime Minister. When questioned, the man said that he had paid a million US dollars for the passport. That raised alarm bells which ultimately resulted in Canada imposing visa requirements for nationals of St. Kitts and Nevis to travel to that country. It raised alarms in St Kitts and Nevis too because the government had never said that it sold diplomatic passports as part of the Citizenship by Investment Programme (CBI). The understandable action taken by Canada damaged the CBI Programme and the good name of the country. The country was told that the man had consular status as representative to Azerbaijan. Most people in St. Kitts and Nevis haven't a clue where Azerbaijan is and there has been no indication of trade or other significant relations between the two countries. The United States has disclosed that Iranians carrying St. Kitts and Nevis passports have, via investments in Georgia, sought to evade US sanctions on Iran. That revelation also embarrassed the country and put the CBI Programme at risk.

Questions remain unanswered as to whether the man did pay for the passport as he said, if so who he paid, whether the sale of diplomatic passports was part of the CBI Programme, how many other such passports have been issued and to whom. That type of information should be subject to freedom of information requests.

The people of a country are entitled to know who its representatives are around the world. Hopefully, these questions will be answered in the future but there are no means available to the public of compelling answers. Hopefully also, the country will be told which locals who are not employed by the government in its diplomatic service carry or carried diplomatic passports. Until then, the situation leaves a very bad taste in the mouths of thinking nationals who now have the cost and inconvenience of applying for visas to travel to Canada and face suspicion across the world by virtue of their nationality. The only comfort I have is the knowledge that a diplomatic passport does not give diplomatic immunity, that is, protection from arrest and prosecution by another country, to any holder of such passport except one actually accredited to the other country. Such passport may be a revenue generator and a status symbol but it is not the shield which many people think it is.

Freedom of Information legislation would help to promote democracy and less secretive governance in St. Kitts and Nevis. However, it is by no means the panacea that some like to think that it could be. Firstly, the list of exemptions will be wide. Secondly, a public authority that wishes to be obstructive can drag out the disclosure process. Thirdly, the process can be time consuming and costly for the citizen. Fourthly, not many citizens have the courage to take on the government in this way. Fifthly, it is not easy in a small society such as ours to find persons who can effectively and with full independence fill the role of Information Commissioner. The legislation is therefore a good tool but not a substitute for a general change of culture to enlightened governance. Nor is it a substitute for general vigilance on the part of the public to combat a lack of transparent governance.

St. Kitts and Nevis needs much more than Freedom of Information legislation. It needs fact and issue based politics. It needs the government-owned *ZIZ TV* and radio stations to be run professionally and to be open to all views with equal access by all political parties and by civil society. It needs a change in mentality in the civil service to promote openness and access. It needs to change the system of appointments to public boards to include competent people regardless of political affiliation. It needs the C.F. Bryant College to develop an effective research arm so that facts are readily available and published. It needs civil society to demand these things.

THE OFFICIAL GAZETTE AND OTHER GOVERNMENT PUBLICATIONS

It is the height of irony that the late publication of the Boundaries Report should have been central to the failure of the scheme to change the electoral boundaries immediately before the 2015 Election.

The constitution provides by section 42 as follows in relation to the Gazette:

> No law made by Parliament shall come into operation until it has been published in the Gazette....

The Gazette containing the new boundaries was not available to the public until January 20, 2015 four days after the government claimed it had been published. As a result, the Assembly having been dissolved on the January 16, 2015, the new boundaries could not, as planned, take effect for the election of February 16, 2015. Something as supposedly simple as making a piece of paper available in a government office tripped up the grand design.

But, timely publication of the Gazette has been haphazard since 1983. It has often not been available on request and has been consistently sent to subscribers months late. As a result the country has been too often in ignorance of the very laws which are meant to govern it. Likewise with government policy; it has not been the practice to routinely publish policies. Policies are mostly heard when pronounced by ministers of government to tout how well they are doing. The practice has been to hold them close to the chest in case the official has to change them or make an exception.

Government departments even hide documents from each other. I give an example. In December 2009, when the National Competitiveness Council (NCC) was appointed it asked for copies of all reports which government had relating to the competitiveness of the country. The NCC was told by the government representatives assigned to collaborate with it that there were none. The Council proceeded to publish its first report in 2010 which is contained in an appendix to this book. After publication of the report, the Council was handed by a government representative an extensive Competitiveness Review and Benchmarking Study on the country done by USAID in 2008. When I was invited to present the NCC report to government I pointed out the existence of the USAID report and expressed the disappointment of the NCC that it had not been made available earlier. No minister present appeared to have heard of that report.

CIVIL SERVICE REFORM

Legislation is required to make the public service more accountable and productive and to deter corruption. Civil Servants at management level should be allowed to manage without constant interference on a day to day basis from politicians and their henchmen. The country needs to develop a model which suits its size and other realities. At the core of that model should be the independence and impartiality of the members of the civil service and a recognition of the role of the civil service heads as executives and, with their management and staff, implementers of policy established by the cabinet or minister.

PROCUREMENT AND OTHER FINANCIAL OVERSIGHT

St. Kitts and Nevis would benefit from a review of this critical area of regulation. The banks and other financial institutions are regulated but oversight is minimal of government and its entities. Regulation by election should not be the only form.

The work of institutions and individuals (including the Director of Audit) who exercise oversight duties should be properly funded and they should be insulated in tenure and remuneration as are the judges. Investigative and enforcement powers should be akin to those of the courts.

The powers of the Director of Audit of oversight of the public purse should be expanded to include oversight of the award of government contracts. I use the words 'public purse' in the widest sense to mean not only the Consolidated Fund but all public monies however called and by whomever managed. The Director of Audit should have a budget which allows him to hire the best available staff and to engage outside auditing and forensic accounting help where necessary. The budget should allow him to establish and maintain a separate office and his own staff. He should be given power to publish periodic and special reports when he considers necessary.

ANTI-CORRUPTION MEASURES

The problem of corruption in small states was well put in perspective by Greg Christie, attorney at law and former Contractor General of Jamaica in a presentation in early 2014 to the Transparency Institute of Trinidad and Tobago and I quote:

> I say this because it is important for us to understand that although corruption is a global problem which impacts both rich and poor countries alike, the threat that it poses to developing countries is disproportionately severe and, if not checked, can potentially lead to state failure or even state capture.

> Indeed, it was Mr. Jim Yong Kim, the President of the World Bank, who incisively characterized the gravity of the matter when, on December 19, 2013, he put it this way: "Let us not mince words. In the developing world, corruption is Public Enemy #1".

> Defined generally as the abuse of public office for private gain, corruption, first and foremost, erodes the quality of life of the citizenry by diverting public funds away from the provision of critical social necessities, such

as health-care, education, water, roads and electricity.

Corruption also leads to human rights violations, steals political elections, distorts financial markets, reduces investor confidence, increases the price of goods and services, undermines or destroys confidence in critical public institutions, and enables organized crime, terrorism and other threats to human security to flourish.

But for developing countries, such as our regional states, the magnitude of the potential for the adverse socio-economic consequences which corruption portends can be substantial.

Insidious in its very nature and in the way in which it operates, the threat of corruption for the Caribbean is foremost in its so-called 'grand' forms. Bribery, kickbacks, embezzlement of public funds, cronyism, links between politicians and organized criminal elements, influence peddling, and the abuse of one's public office for political gain, or to pervert the course of justice, are but a few of its far-reaching manifestations which should be of major concern to us in the region.

St. Kitts and Nevis accepts immigrants, investors and new citizens from countries in which corruption is embedded or in which it is the norm to pay government officials for favours. Very few of these countries have legislation like the 'Foreign Corrupt Practices Act' in the USA which forbids US citizens from engaging in corrupt practices anywhere in the world. It would be naïve to assume that all of the immigrants, investors and citizens will drop their national habits. Many of these persons have lots of money. The combination of that factor and the lack of clear, detailed and enforceable rules to ensure accountability and transparency in our governance and the political partisanship and the patronage and entitlements mentality springing from it and the huge amounts of money spent on election campaigns have put St. Kitts and Nevis at risk of corruption becoming embedded and perhaps even public enemy number one (to borrow the language of the World Bank chief). If that happens our democracy will be at even greater risk.

There is a strong perception of corruption in the decimation of the SIDF described in chapter 3 and in some of the other shenanigans associated with the CBI. There will no doubt be full revelations in due course.

The country needs to address this issue frontally and effectively.

STRENGTHENING CIVIL SOCIETY

A country is only as strong as its civil society. Too many groups within civil society in our islands are silent. At the same time the politicians are becoming better and better at spin with the aid of highly paid spin doctors from around the world.

I am interested by the rise of nontraditional civil society groups like Transparency Institute in Trinidad and National Integrity Action in Jamaica. Some of these groups are affiliated with international organisations. St. Kitts and Nevis needs branches of international groups like these and more think tanks to raise the level of discourse. Individual members of the society and groups within it should consider joining organisations of this type and establishing local chapters.

PUBLIC BOARDS

Many government services are no longer provided by the civil service but by statutory corporations and other government appointed or controlled commissions, authorities, companies and entities. I refer to these as public boards. The rationale for this type of institution is, while retaining ultimate government oversight, to improve efficiencies and flexibility in the operation of the services entrusted to them and to avoid the type of red tape and bureaucracy which is associated with the work of the civil service. In practice most public boards in St. Kitts and Nevis have operated exactly like the civil service. The same review and remodeling is required as I have recommended for the civil service.

Here is a commentary I did on March 23, 2015.

In our tribal culture, with a change of government comes changes in some if not most boards. A position on a public board is too often regarded as a plum for big supporters and a form of reward for persons who worked hard for the election of their candidate. Such appointments carry pay and perks. They carry power to hire and fire and to make important decisions. As a result they carry prestige. Not much thought is given to the responsibilities which come with the money and the perks and the power and the prestige.

Before I proceed let me refer to the Four Seasons Accord which is the name given to the national agreement made in November 1994 between all political parties in the Federation and civil society organisations to resolve the disputes and violence which arose from the 1993 general election.

The Accord called for "a complete review of the system of appointments to Government Commissions, Boards, Corporations, Authorities and other agencies with a view to establishing greater independence and efficiency in the operation of these bodies"

That agreement has not been honoured by any government since. Loyalty to the party in power has for the most part remained the first qualification for appointment. Loyalty has superceded the requirements of skill, knowledge, independence and competence.

In the hope that the new Government will not fall into the same trap I offer a commentary on some of the responsibilities which come with the position.

In the case of statutory bodies the duty of the director is owed to the country and not to the minister or the cabinet. The board of a statutory corporation is entrusted with power and publicly owned assets and charged with operating the relevant enterprise or service in accordance with the empowering statute and the national interest. Thus while cabinet or the minister may appoint the board and dictate policy, directors are required to exercise their own judgment in implementing the policy. If that were not the case there would be no need for a board. In other words a board is not a rubber stamp.

In the case of a government owned or controlled company the duty of the director is owed to the company as a whole and not to the government or any minister. To give a simple example, if government were to apply for a loan from National Bank the directors have to detach themselves from their politics and consider first and foremost whether the loan is commercially viable and in the best interests of the bank. They must exercise their duty in that way regardless of the fact that government voted its majority shares in the bank to appoint them. Their duty is owed to all two thousand plus shareholders and to the bank's thousands of depositors, not just the government.

A director must know the powers given to him and the board by the statute, in the case of a statutory body, or the Articles of Association, in the case of a company. That seems to go without saying but my experience is that many directors do not know and do not consult the documents until there is a problem. Sometimes that can be too late.

The board of a statutory body or government controlled company which is engaged in business activities e.g the Port Authority, NHC, SKELEC, The Cable, National Bank, ZIZ generally has oversight of the business of the entity. The board in most instances appoints management which runs the business on a day to day basis. Management so appointed should be carefully and independently selected and should be capable of running the entity. Unless a director is given managerial powers he or she should let management run the business subject to the oversight of the board. Too often directors think they have power to intervene in day to day decisions. That often frustrates and hinders management. What if six directors were to give six different directions. That just could not work. A board is not supposed to micro-manage a business. Some directors try to show their power and to compensate for their lack of competence to do their real job by trying to delve into day to day decisions. That is where allegations of political interference often arise.

Unless a statute says so there is no requirement that a director have any specific qualification, degree or profession. The standard is generally that the director act honestly and in good faith with a view to the best interests of the entity and that he or she exercise the care, diligence and skill that a reasonably prudent person would exercise in comparable circumstances. That is the definition in the Companies Act which would apply to most statutory bodies as well. Directors may have different skills and different areas of expertise. That can be helpful in providing a balance on the board. There is however one skill which every director of an entity, public or private, carrying on business must have and that is a basic understanding of accounts.

How otherwise can a person properly direct the entity? If the director does not have that knowledge it means that he or she will not know how the company is doing financially and will be unable to participate properly in review of the operations of the entity or in financial decisions and planning. It will mean that management or other directors can fool him or her. Each director must participate in those key areas. A director abdicates his duty if he simply leaves such decisions up to others on the board. A person who cannot read accounts is not suited to appointment to any public board which is required to provide an account of its finances.

A conflict of interest may arise between the interest of the entity and the personal interest of a director. The general rule is that the interest of the entity must prevail and a director will be liable to cough up any benefit he or she received if the director preferred his personal interest. Personal in this case includes political. A director should be familiar with the rules which apply to his or her disclosure of conflicts or potential conflicts.

Conflicts can exist which make a person unsuitable for a position on a public board. For example you would not expect a director of a major trading company in St. Kitts or Nevis to be appointed to the board of National Bank.

That could give him or her access to the accounts and confidential information of his competitors which would be improper. You would not expect a building contractor or a building materials supplier to be appointed to the board of NHC. Likewise an architect or engineer or other construction professional who submits applications to the Development Control and Planning Board should not be a member of that board. Even though he can recuse himself from participating in decisions of the board relating to his applications, his membership of the board will give him intimate knowledge of plans presented by his competitors. It also gives the impression that he or she is in a position to exert influence on the board. Appearances of conflict can be as damaging as actual conflict and should be avoided.

It should go without saying that a director must maintain confidentiality in respect of information which he receives in his role. He must not even disclose that information to the political directorate. If the information is such that it should be reported to the political directorate then the reporting should come via the board. If that principle were adhered to we would have less accusations of directors being appointed as spies.

Finally, a word on the Chairman of a board. The Chairman may have duties assigned to him by the statute or the Articles of a company over and above his duties as a director. The board may assign additional duties to him. If that is not the case then the Chairman has no greater powers than another director. I am constrained to make those statements because the culture has developed in respect of public boards that the Chairman is the Grand Chief and has power to control the board and to run the entity. That is an unfortunate culture and has contributed to political interference and the lack of independence of many public boards. I am not casting aspersions on any particular Chair of a public board but speaking of the public perception.

I have by no means exhausted this topic but I hope I have said enough to warn the new government and their supporters that public boards are not their property to do with as they see fit and there is a responsibility to the country to appoint the best people available regardless of party or political persuasion. And the people appointed are not expected to act as surrogates of the political directorate but as independent thinkers and decision makers within the powers given to them.

I hope also that the government will follow the laws governing statutory corporations in tabling in the National Assembly the accounts of those entities. It should go further and, even if not required by law, publish the accounts and ample reports on the activities of each entity. It should also publish auditors' reports. Only then will government usher in the new dispensation and the real change, to which its members have committed, of greater accountability and transparency.

I hope too that this will be a word to the wise as our citizens are becoming more aware of their rights and are less fearful of enforcing them. Our courts are becoming more innovative in creating effective remedies for public wrongs. It behoves therefore those who seek positions as board members to think carefully of their legal responsibilities and potential financial liabilities in taking such positions.

10. *Economic Development*

The economy of St. Kitts was centred on the sugar industry for over 350 years until 2005 when, after more than three decades of heavy subsidization while in government hands, the industry was closed. The industry had been closed in Nevis more than half a century earlier.

St. Kitts moved into light manufacturing in the late 1960s. That sector remains as a moderately significant contributor in terms of jobs and exports despite carrying higher wages than Haiti and Mexico and other low-cost producing countries. Both islands have also attracted offshore universities and offer offshore financial services in varying degrees.

There have been substantial improvements in infrastructure development on both islands. Roads, airports, seaports, communications and utilities have all received heavy investment.

Both islands were late into tourism as compared to other Caribbean islands. The profile of both islands as tourism destinations has grown and foreign direct investment in the industry is promising. There is great potential in the country's tourism industry but that potential is yet to be fulfilled. Much must be done to achieve that potential.

In 1980 the country introduced an unorthodox but effective tax regime which has remained largely intact since and has helped to attract local and foreign investment and long term residents. Income tax on individuals is charged at relatively low rates on wages and salaries and on gross revenues from unincorporated businesses and professions carried on in the country. Interest and dividends earned and capital gains made by resident individuals are not taxed. There are no death duties nor inheritance tax. Corporations doing business locally pay tax on net profits (current rate 33 per cent). VAT was introduced in 2010. Stamp duties on the transfer of property (except between parents and children which are nominal) are comparatively high. The general rates at May 2015 are 5 per cent of the price or market value whichever is higher on the sale of condominiums, 2.5 per cent on the sale of timeshare interests and 10 per cent on the sale of other real property.

As noted previously, the country's creditors generously forgave a large part of the massive national debt. The severe effects of the world recession post 2008 have to a degree been cushioned by that relief and by revenues from investments (more commonly known abroad as passport sales) under the Citizenship by Investment Programme (CBI). Under the CBI, an investor of a minimum of US$400,000 in an approved non-government investment or by a direct, non-refundable contribution of US$250,000 (or more for families) to the Government via the SIDF can, if he passes character checks, be granted citizenship and a passport. The application of a male adult can cover his spouse and minor children and those undergoing full time education. The spouse and children also receive passports. An investor making the qualifying non-government investment also pays substantial fees to government and stamp duty on qualifying property purchases.

Initially only properties of new construction in the tourism sector qualified as investments under the CBI. However, post-2010 the CBI went off the rails. All sorts of properties have been approved as investments, including private homes, small apartments and rundown commercial properties, as the programme became lax and was abused, resulting in embarrassment for the good name of the country. Following the 26 Month Election the CBI is being reviewed.

The economic development of St. Kitts and Nevis has been stymied by lack of social cohesion, the dysfunctional politics of which I have lamented and the resulting entitlements mentality. Successive governments have ignored the social discipline and productivity required for successful economic development. They have forgotten the importance of social capital in the economic development of the country. St. Kitts and Nevis has had no cohesive or comprehensive or long term development model. It's development has been too largely pursued on a reactive and short term basis influenced more by the electoral cycle than by long term considerations.

There has been no realistic plan to prepare our people for the tourism industry. As a result, the standards of service are at best variable. Recommendations for the establishment of a full hotel school with public/private partnership were ignored. Recommendations for promoting a culture of excellence in service were likewise dismissed. That culture does not mix well with the prevailing culture of handouts. No real attempt has been made to address the declining attitudes and social discipline. Low levels of productivity generally have been ignored.

There has never been a master plan for tourism. There has never been any real vision as to the type of tourist destination the country wishes to be. Hotel and other tourism projects were accepted sporadically as and when they came along. The focus in tourism was sometimes said to be aimed at the five star market. Any hope of that fell away with the development of one star properties in the feeding frenzy that became the CBI Programme.

There have been no benchmarks indicated by government for the CBI programme in terms of the number of properties to be approved as qualifying investments and the number of citizenships to be issued under the programme. One developer, sensing the free for all environment, boasted that he would build 5000 units. Planning regulation of developments under the programme has been haphazard leaving the country with eyesores that may in future best be used as homeless shelters. These monstrosities will have a very negative impact on property values throughout St. Kitts.

The tax regime referred to and the growth of offshore education services and the restriction in the amount of campus housing which universities are allowed to build incentivized many locals to build apartments or to add apartments to their homes. Many of these apartments now lie empty because several of the buildings constructed under the CBI programme have been rented as student accommodation. The CBI programme has thereby become counter productive to property development by ordinary Kittitians.

Cruise shipping was attracted because of Port Zante. Port Zante was the idea of the enterprising Matalon family of Jamaica who built the port and reclaimed 34 acres of land for cruise ship related business. It was at first greeted with skepticism and opposition from many who never thought it would work. It will attract close to a million cruise ship passengers in the current year.

The country moved into offshore education services thanks in large measure to the coincidental arrival of Dr. Robert Ross. The country should be eternally grateful to the vision and business acumen of Dr. Ross in establishing Ross University School of Veterinary Medicine in 1983 and the University of Medicine and Health Sciences and the International University of Nursing between 2004 and 2007. Dr. Ross put the country on the map of attractive locations for offshore schools.

The country has (Nevis from 1984 and St. Kitts from 1996) held itself out as a provider of offshore financial services but only Nevis has pursued this seriously. St. Kitts' offshore financial services have never been properly marketed.

There has been no known policy on the importation of labour from outside the region. People have moved into the country from Asian countries without effective controls and limits. There are Asian shop assistants and tradesmen and labourers while the government spends tens of millions each year in grants to keep local youth employed. The traditional family village shop is now almost extinct. If the work ethic is not improved more foreigners will come in to work in the tourism sector.

There has been no plan for the involvement of the diaspora in the development of the country, except of course for voting purposes. Very few of the many educated and talented second and third generation nationals are attracted to the country. These are the scores of thousands whom the late Sir Lee Moore referred to as talent in exile.

There is no comprehensive legal regime for incentivizing development. Incentives have been in many instances negotiated on an ad hoc basis. Many of the incentives granted to developers exceed the limits set by law. The law incentivizing hotel development remains the ancient Hotels Aid Act of 1956.

There has been so much talk about the conservation and exploitation as a tourism asset of beautiful Basseterre but no plan has emerged for that worthwhile goal. To its credit, the Nevis Government is beautifying Charlestown.

St. Kitts has some of the most fertile soil in the world. It was known by the Carib Indians as *Liamuiga*, the Fertile Land. The government owns most of the fertile land. No zoning plan has been published for use of that land and its potential for agriculture has been minimally exploited. No policy has been stated regarding large scale farming which is highly feasible alongside the traditional small farms. The huge potential in agriculture is yet to be realized.

Despite all the grand talk, there is no plan to make the country business friendly. As a result the rankings of the country in the yearly World Bank *Doing Business Report* have declined alarmingly over the past six years despite the World Bank providing the Government in 2009 with a reform paper containing recommendations for making the country more business friendly. The *Doing Business Report* ranks the business environment in countries across the world. The higher the ranking the more friendly is the assessment of the business climate. Here are the rankings for St. Kitts and Nevis from 2006 to 2015:

2006	–	85
2007	–	85
2008	–	64
2009	–	70
2010	–	76
2011	–	84
2012	–	95
2013	–	96
2014	–	101
2015	–	121

The numbers speak for themselves - a drop of 51 places in the last 6 years.

In a country heavily reliant on foreign investment generally and on investment in property under the CBI, the time taken to get a title to property has become inordinately longer and longer because the Title Registry is operated the same way as it was 50 years ago. Twenty years ago a month would be regarded as a long time to get a title registered. Now six months is not unusual. This is one of the categories in which the countries are separately ranked in the Doing Business Report. In 2015 the ranking of St. Kitts and Nevis in that category was, appallingly, 170 out of 189 countries.

Backlogs are also normal in the CBI office which has taken longer and longer to process applications or has done so selectively, this in the face of increasing competition from other countries in the region and outside. This inefficiency has put the CBI at risk.

Every country should have a long term vision or model for its economic and social development. That is all the more important for a small country with limited resources in a globalized and highly competitive world. St. Kitts and Nevis should have such vision and create a plan and goals for implementing the vision. The vision may have to be adapted as circumstances change. The plan and goals will be subject to constant review but they should exist. The people of the country should know what they are and should be supportive of them. The world should know what the vision is.

The shining example of a small country which has succeeded in this way is Singapore, an island state with limited land mass, no natural resources and a volatile political past. Singapore is roughly the size of St. Lucia with a population (at June 2014) of 5.46 million including 3.34 million citizens, 0.53 million permanent residents and 1.60 million temporary residents including students. In 1965 amid political unrest and violence Singapore was thrown out of the Federation of Malaysia and became an independent republic. Very few people gave it much of a chance but, pursuing the vision of its dynamic leader Lee Kuan Yew, that country rose in a single generation from an impoverished Third World trading outpost to a wealthy, internationally admired First World country. That success was based on the simple tenets of strong social discipline and order, meritocracy, a business friendly environment, efficient government and civil service, strong productivity and work ethic, zero corruption, multi-racialism and an education system geared to these objectives. Singapore assiduously pursued its plans to give effect to its chosen model. As a result and against large odds it enjoyed an average GDP growth rate of 6.79 per cent between 1976 and 2014, an amazing accomplishment. It is one of the most orderly, competitive and efficient countries in the world. Singapore ranks consistently first in the "Doing Business Index".

I dislike the authoritarian manner used by Lee Quan Yew and the government of Singapore but that suited the culture of Singaporeans who bought into the model and accepted it. St. Kitts and Nevis would do well to pursue the basic components of the Singapore model without the authoritarian method. All of those components are attainable with a clear vision, social cohesion and with responsible and enterprising leadership. Because of its more open society and different culture, St. Kitts and Nevis may not be able to achieve as much social discipline as has Singapore but substantially improved social discipline and productivity can be achieved if that goal is seriously and systematically pursued. The change can occur without changing the natural friendliness of the people and their open spirit which are positives in tourism.

I do not intend to belittle the advances made nor to understate the problems faced but there can be little argument that the country would have advanced further had there been established long term goals with the people unified in support of them and had development been pursued systematically rather than in response to the demands of short term politics. The term sustainable development has been a buzz word for years but there is no long term plan to achieve this. It is not too late to create a vision and plan but the country is at crossroads as a result of not having them.

Cruise Ships at Port Zante, St.Kitts

Castle in a residential area

Development on side of a ghaut

Ugly development on scenic hillside

Warehouse on a major beach

11. *The Social Contract*

Society is a group of human beings living in a defined space in an organised community. The basis of civilized society is an agreement (widely called the social contract) which prevails within the community, that the people will live peacefully together in an orderly manner according to a set of rules. To that end the people agree to assume certain responsibilities, to co-operate for the common good, to share some of their belongings and income, to give up certain freedoms and to curb certain human instincts for the common good and development of the society and for its security, peace and good order.

A key element of the social contract is the entrusting of power to a government whose members are expected to represent the interests of the society in general in priority to personal interests or the interests of any section of the society. The government is empowered to make just and fair laws. The government is also entrusted with the exercise of executive power to provide social services, infrastructure and security and to pursue the social and economic development of the society. The government is entrusted with public revenue to execute that mandate. Checks and balances should exist to prevent abuse by government of this enormous power. Those checks and balances should be enforced by an independent justice system which should also resolve disputes between members of society.

The terms of the social contract evolve with time and changes in circumstances. Habits change, norms change, the culture changes. It is important however that the evolution does not occur on a purely reactive basis. A society should chart the development of its social norms as much as it does its economic growth. This requires active engagement by the society in discussing the factors which influence its development and in countering those which are negative. The society should also discuss positive ways of influencing its development. Too often in St. Kitts and Nevis the discussion is reactive. It centers too much on individuals and not issues. This to some extent is reflective of the past. It reflects a lack of self confidence in ourselves as a people. To get over this weakness, the people must recognize it as a weakness and actively engage in reversing it.

A society which takes the social contract and its stability for granted or which tolerates its abuse does so at its peril. Like any contract and any relationship, the parties, in this case the members of society, must work at implementation of the contract and must guard its norms and interests. To do so the members or sections of the society, including civil society and the education sector, must be consciously and constantly engaged with the government and with each other in debate on the execution of the social contract and on improvements which can be made to it.

Human nature makes the social contract a complex operation and often militates against its effective implementation. As a nation founded on the belief in God, St. Kitts and Nevis as a society is meant to espouse love as the governing principle. St. Paul says *while knowledge puffs up love is what builds*. That principle is not however applied in practice as much as it should be. Instead the negative human instincts too often prevail.

The motto 'Principles not men' of my old school the St. Kitts-Nevis Grammar School (and still the motto of its successor the Basseterre High School) is very relevant. I am not saying that men are not important. The quality of men and women is critical to the implementation of the social contract. But the interests of individual men and women should not supercede principles. A society which ignores principles and glorifies men puts its social contract at risk.

How do the people of St. Kitts and Nevis stand in adherence to their social contract? The answer in short is not very well at present.

I have sought earlier in this book to show the weaknesses in our governance system and the abuses of that system. I have sought to show how that has affected the interaction of the people. Both are key elements of the social contract which require substantial changes and improvement and with which no right thinking person can be satisfied.

I turn next to crime. The levels of crime and particularly crime involving violence have grown enormously since the turn of the century. In the 1960s and 1970s few if any of the three criminal assizes in St. Kitts and two in Nevis ever lasted as long as a month. In 2014 the High Court could sit year round and not have time to hear all the criminal cases. The case load of the Magistrates Court has also increased significantly.

I recall at least one occasion in the 1970s when there were no cases at all to be tried at the criminal assizes in Nevis. The practice then was to hold the parade of police (traditional at the commencement of assizes) outside the Court House and then to present the judge with a pair of white gloves reflecting the purity of the community.

Murders were rare. One in a year was regarded as a bad year. In the last fifteen years, in a country of less than 50,000, there have been more than a total of two hundred with a peak in 2011 of thirty five. The number in 2014 was twenty three. There have been 16 for the year up to June 2015. That is a rate per annum in excess of 60 per 100,000 of population, one of the highest rates in the world. That rate is ten times the rate in the U.S.A. According to a Global Study on Homicide 2013 published by the UN Office on Drugs and Crime, St. Kitts and Nevis (with 18 homicides) had the 8th highest murder rate in the world. A rate of 23 per year would result in half of one per cent of the population being killed in a decade. That would be the equivalent in the United States of 1,500,000 murders per decade which would be regarded as a disaster. The brutal nature, brazenness and impunity of many of the murders disgrace St. Kitts and Nevis as a civilized country. Many of them are executions. This in a country where, according to its national anthem, *"peace abounds."*

What are the reasons for this? Before I address that I think it important to highlight the differences between St. Kitts and Nevis in 1967 and in 2015. In 1967 living conditions were very basic for the majority of people. Very few people owned land or their home. The infrastructure was modest. There were two High Schools in St. Kitts one for less than 500 boys and one for a couple hundred girls. There was one Sixth Form in St. Kitts and Nevis. Students from Nevis who wished to do *"A"* Levels (now CAPE) had to move to St. Kitts. There was no college. There was a handful of doctors. The airport, or more appropriately the airfield, in St. Kitts consisted of one small building and a short runway which was unable to take jet planes. You had to go to Antigua to catch one of those. Ships docked in the stream of the Basseterre harbour and cargo was landed by barges. Passengers alighted by small boats. There were a few hundred vehicles, now there are more than ten thousand. Except for those who emigrated to England, the USA, Canada and the Virgin Islands and students who went away to study, very few people traveled at all and most of those who did, traveled within the Caribbean.

There was no television. I first saw a television set in England when I was 18 years old. Telephone service was by landline only and few people could afford the service. Cable and Wireless operated a very limited international calling service. Urgent messages were sent by telegram. Cell phones were not invented. Communication for the most part was by mail. It took seven days for a letter to come from St. Thomas, seven to ten from the U.S.A and four to seven from Britain. There were no fax machines and no computers. There were no calculators. There were cumbersome adding machines to supplement the brain. There were no electric typewriters. There were no photocopiers. In terms of appliances there were no washing machines. That was a chore done by hand. There were no microwave ovens. There were no vacuum cleaners. There were very few hot water heaters. There were very few gadgets to help in cooking and cleaning. The first computer I saw was when I was checking in with BA to return home from my studies in 1971. The computer took up an entire room. It probably had less capacity than most cell phones now have.

Substantial improvements have been achieved in living and economic conditions since 1967. Technology has made life more comfortable and provided more leisure time for most people. Higher education is much more readily available than it was then. Health care, if not world class, is better and more readily available than it was. The infrastructure of ports, roads, electricity and services is far better. Sporting facilities are light years ahead of what they were. Television has exposed the world to us. And incidentally there is a greater number of churches now although I am unable to say whether more people go to church.

These facts beg the question - do improvements in economic conditions automatically lead to more crime? The answer is not necessarily. What then has taken St. Kitts and Nevis from a country where no one locked his or her car and few their homes; where there were no burglar bars or alarm systems or security cameras or security guards; where you could safely travel to or walk in any part of the country at any time of the day or night; where the village contributed to the upbringing of children; where teachers were revered and respected by children and parents? What caused some of the international media to label St. Kitts as 'Devil's Island' in the early 1990s. What has caused St. Kitts and Nevis to have one of the highest murder rates per capita in the world? What has led to young men being gunned down on the beaches where most of the world dream of enjoying? What has led to the need for the security forces armed with machine guns and with back-up on call to be on hand to protect residents and visitors who want to enjoy the unique pleasures of the Strip at Frigate Bay? What has led to one of the highest rates of incarceration in the world? A prison built for 80 inmates that was never full in the 1960s and 1970s is now overflowing with over 350 prisoners most of them young, healthy men. Why are we unable as a society to rally around the police and give them strong and unified support as they confront the problems of crime, instead of politicizing their work? What on earth has led to the police finding it necessary to search every student in a high school in investigating a threat to the Head Teacher? Why should our healthcare workers have to fear for their lives as a murder was committed in the emergency room of our main hospital? Why should a Justice of the Supreme Court of the USA, or any tourist for that matter, not be able to holiday in Nevis without being robbed? Why should a school girl on her way to Church not be able to reach there without being raped and murdered in a public bath?

In May 2010 the National Competitiveness Council sent a resolution to the Prime Minister pointing out the grave effect that crime could have on the development of the country. The resolution set out some of the factors influencing the crime wave. These are set out below.

- Gangs and misguided youth

- Deportees

- Easy availability of illegal weapons

- Limited male role models

- Children having children

- Poor parenting

- Disappearance of "community parenting"

- Political tribalism

- Weak law enforcement and crime detection

- Lack of public confidence in and co-operation with the police

- Violence on television, the internet, video games and other electronic devices

- Increased tolerance of violence generally

- Other negative influences on youth
- Imported habits
- Decline in respect for the law
- Decline in discipline generally
- Inadequate attention to low achievers in the education system
- Decline in spiritual pursuits
- Inhumane prison facilities
- Lack of correctional facilities for young offenders

There may well be more than the 20 causes listed and these causes are not stated in order of priority.

Many of these factors speak for themselves. They indicate fundamental deficiencies in the concepts and implementation of the social contract, key elements of which are the nurturing and education of the young. In my opinion poor parenting and lack of male role models are key factors. Men are being left behind generally by women except in politics. Negative attitudes as outlined in the list are also a key factor. So is the lack of co-operation by the communities with the police.

Often ignored as a factor are the prison conditions. These are a disgrace to a civilized society. They constitute a breach of the fundamental right of prisoners not to be subjected to inhuman and degrading punishment. They breach all international standards of punishment. They perpetuate rather than deter crime.

If the factors outlined are not reversed or abated then the society will produce generation after generation of delinquent young men. The entire society, not only the government and the police force, must play a role in the solution.

Violent crime is not the only crime of note. Theft, including theft from employers and white collar theft is too prevalent. Corruption has reared its ugly head in the society. These too are affected by societal attitudes.

The problem of crime is a very complex one. There are no easy answers and no short term fixes. However, I am certain that if as a society the people of St. Kitts and Nevis were to put their politics aside and address the social issues facing the country in a positive and unified and responsible manner they would find some of the solutions. I also know that if the issues are not so addressed the country puts its progress at serious risk.

To progress, a society has to learn from history. Our history was one of abuse, exploitation and domination until self governance in 1967. Even when they ceded some measure of local control, the British colonialists practiced divide and rule. That has been inculcated into the psyche of leadership and has remained the norm. The people have for the most part unwittingly accepted that. The country needs to purge itself of that culture and not allow its leaders to mimic the colonial British for their personal gain. The extent to which people worship leaders is a clear reflection of this. The degree to which people want to destroy each other shows likewise. The time has come for people to realise that leaders are there to serve not rule. Humility should replace arrogance as the tenet of leadership. Civility should replace abuse as the prevailing method of interaction. Only then will the society be able to address the social problems it faces.

In summary the society which addresses constantly and honestly and frontally the impact which human foibles can have on the social contract stands a better chance of achieving balance and good order in the implementation of the contract.

Roman Catholic Co-Cathedral Basseterre, St. Kitts

The Great House, Ottleys Plantation Inn, St.Kitts

Fairview, St Kitts

Brimstone Hill, St. Kitts

Romney Manor, St. Kitts

12. *Caribbean Integration*

Although, as noted in the chapter on the revolt in Anguilla, the West Indies Federation failed and the Little Eight did not materialize, the leaders of the West Indies did not, to their credit, give up on regional integration. In 1965 The Caribbean Free Trade Area (CARIFTA) was established to promote trade between the member countries. It began with four countries but by 1971 had grown to twelve. Its main objective was to encourage balanced development of the region by promoting free trade and industrial development. In 1973, by the Treaty of Chaguaramas, CARIFTA morphed into the Caribbean Community (CARICOM) with a wider remit.

In 1981 seven Eastern Caribbean States entered into the Treaty of Basseterre establishing the sub-regional Organisation of Eastern Caribbean States (OECS). The member states of the OECS have continued their membership of Caricom. In 2011, The OECS countries moved to strengthen their relationship and functional co-operation by the revision of the Treaty of Basseterre to create an economic union.

The purposes of the revised OECS Treaty of Basseterre are set out in the treaty as follows:

- to promote co-operation among the Member States and at the regional and international levels having due regard to the Revised Treaty of Chaguaramas and the Charter of the United Nations;

- to maintain unity and solidarity among the Member States and the defence of their sovereignty, territorial integrity and independence;

- to assist the Member States in the realisation of their obligations and responsibilities to the international community with due regard to the role of international law as a standard of conduct in their relationship;

- to seek to achieve the fullest possible harmonisation of foreign policy among the Member States, to seek to adopt wherever possible, common positions on international issues, and to establish and maintain, wherever possible, arrangements for joint overseas representation and common services;

- to establish the Economic Union as a single economic and financial space;

- to be an institutional forum to discuss and facilitate constitutional, political and economic changes necessary for the successful development of Member States and their successful participation in the regional and global economies;

- to pursue the said purposes through its respective Institutions and Organs by discussion of questions of common concern for the Member States and by agreement and common action.

It is to be noted that these purposes are wide enough to have justified intervention, or at the very least strong pressure, by other OECS countries on the Douglas regime when it delayed in tabling the Motion of No Confidence. While that was happening Douglas was invited to be guest speaker at a political convention of the ruling party of Kenny Anthony in St. Lucia. Anthony himself and Ralph Gonsalves had appeared on the political platform of the Labour party in St. Kitts. Prime Minister Skerritt of Dominica was a known supporter of Douglas. It was not surprising when Gonsalves said in 2013 there was no basis for him to get involved in the MONC controversy because there was no disorder in St. Kitts. It was pleasantly surprising when he and Prime Ministers Mitchell and Skerritt, the last being Chair of the OECS at the time, found their conscience and intervened on the morning after the 2015 election. I suppose better late than never but let's hope that they and their people learn the lesson of their mistaken inaction.

Back to the history. In July 1989 with the challenges of globalization in mind and the new millennium approaching, and presumably dissatisfied with the pace of implementation of the Caricom treaty, the Caricom Heads decided to transform the Common Market into a single market and economy (CSME). They also established the West Indian Commission for Advancing the Goals of the Treaty of Chaguaramas to consult and make recommendations to that end. The Commission comprised fifteen eminent persons from regional countries under the patronage of Dame Nita Barrow and the Chairmanship of Sir Shridath Ramphal with Sir

Alister McIntyre as Vice Chairman. There can be no question that its membership comprised some of the best of regional expertise, experience and wisdom.

The Commission traveled extensively throughout the region and consulted widely with the governments and peoples of all member countries of Caricom at the time as well as members of the Caribbean Diaspora. They invited and considered written submissions. On June 30, 1992 they presented a report to the Caricom Heads of Government that was later published in 1993 in a book of 592 pages entitled *Time for Action*. The report covered every conceivable area in which regional co-operation could be improved and activated.

In his postscript in the book Sir Shridath writes of his address to the opening session of the meeting of Caricom Heads at which the report was to be presented. He expressed in these words the cynicism which the Commission had encountered in its consultations with the people of the region:

> ...but it is a symptom of what ails our regional processes that the most pervasive mood we have encountered among West Indian people is disbelief that anything – anything serious, anything effective, anything lasting, anything fundamentally different, anything that can anchor ambition in a West Indian future – will come out of our efforts and yours. They have grown enured to high flown declarations, they have grown cynical about bureaucratic delays, they have grown disdainful of the instinct to protect small areas of turf leaving the wide West Indian pasture fallow. They will not be surprised if in this time for action you do not act, if at this moment of decision you differ and defer.

He would have done better to quote from the calypso *All we are is just sea water and sand* by Chalkdust who sang of the Caricom Heads:

> And they meeting regularly
> Drawing up all kind of treaty
> And after dey drink dey whiskey
> The treaty dead already
> At the Heads of Government conference
> Is mere shop talk and ignorance
> Lots of talk
> But no action ever commence.

The Commission spoke of the need for more central authority within Caricom and more direct people participation. The Heads were not prepared to accept even the very limited impositions suggested by the Commission on their power and on their fictional notion of sovereignty of their individual countries. They rejected the recommendations of the Commission for a Caricom Commission and for expansion of their proposed Assembly of Parliamentarians to include participation of other social partners. The Commission's recommendation for a Charter of Civil Society was agreed to 'in principle.' The Heads, not unexpectedly, rejected the notion of greater public access to information. Full transparency is anathema to them as is any means of compelling member states to implement the CSME. The recommendation for the Caricom Supreme Court was 'noted.'

It has been argued that, in comparison with the form and depth of integration in other parts of the world (e.g the European Union), the recommendations of the report on greater centralization of executive control of Caricom were inadequate. The European Union comprises peoples who have far less in common than the Caribbean but these peoples, in their social and economic interests, have given up some of their sovereignty for the common good. The Caribbean region of fifteen country members and approximately seven million people with so much in common should be able to integrate more easily than the European Union of twenty eight countries (and growing) and half a billion people speaking dozens of languages.

Of the ten recommendations of a structural nature presented by the Commission to the Caricom Heads they accepted only three namely the need for a revised treaty, the concept of Caricom as a community of sovereign states and the proposal for a Council of Ministers for Caricom Affairs. They accepted many of the non-structural recommendations which did not trouble their turf or sovereignty.

As was expected the Heads did their own thing and took another nine years to revise the Treaty of Chaguaramas, including mechanisms for the CSME. The revised treaty sets out the organs of Caricom but they ignored the recommendations of the Commission for greater centralisation and for more direct people participation and limited the governance of Caricom to Government Heads, their Ministers and their bureaucrats, largely maintaining the status quo in that regard.

Since the revised treaty of 2001 Caricom has, not surprisingly, marked time, due mainly to political intransigence and the 'Chalkdust' syndrome which has also been referred to as 'the region's crippling implementation deficit'. The region is still a long way from achieving the envisaged CSME.

The 'Time For Action' report was not a total waste of time as it has put on record for future generations a guide to what this generation saw as the way forward for the region. Hopefully in future years medication will be developed which cures politicians of the sovereignty and turf disease. It is amazing how the condition afflicts leaders across the Caribbean region, regardless of country or race or background or political party. It is amazing how politicians in opposition criticize the condition but catch its as soon as they win political office.

One area in which some progress has been made is greater movement of peoples within the region. The revised Treaty of Chaguaramas declares free movement to be a goal and provides for some steps towards this, such as movement of skilled nationals. However there is a long way to go towards the goal of full freedom of movement. Some of the people of the region are as much to blame as are their leaders for this. Insularity is still prevalent in some countries as evidenced by the treatment in Barbados of the Jamaican Shanique Myrie which became *a cause celebre* when she took the Barbados Government to the Caribbean Court of Justice and won an award of damages for the suffering and humiliation (including cavity searches) imposed on her by Barbados border agents. The award was token in amount (only Bds$75,000) but reminded the Barbados government of its treaty obligations.

The West Indian Commission recommended that a Caricom Supreme Court be established. As previously noted, in 2001 the Caribbean Court of Justice (CCJ) was established by agreement between Caricom countries.

As disappointing as may be the pace towards regional integration and as superficial as may be the commitment of regional leaders to that integration, the 26 Month Election in St. Kitts and Nevis has awakened the region to the reality that the entire region is affected by crises in any part of it and by damage to the reputation of a single member country. That fact was reflected in the intervention, albeit last minute, of the regional Prime Ministers and in the many editorials and articles in the regional press right after the election. Here are some examples:

> From Caribbean 360.com – *However, going forward, Caricom must look at ways in which they can put pressure on sitting Prime Ministers who behave in the way Douglas did. I know it is the mantra not to get involved in domestic politics. I will say that the politics of any regional country is a domestic issue for Caricom.*

It is my humble opinion that other Prime Ministers should have refused sitting at the same table with Denzil Douglas – a long time ago; he should not have been given that privilege to sit with democratically elected leaders, while he frustrates the democratic process in his own country.

And from an article in the *Nation News* of Barbados headed *ALL AH WE IS ONE*

Indeed the appointment of partisan middle management types, unsuited to neutral national service, has been replicated in several Caribbean countries. The one distinguishing feature of the St. Kitts case was how glaringly the weakness was played out. Despite how tragicomical the St. Kitts election appeared, no Caribbean country should take solace in the false claim that "it cannot happen here". However the real lesson of St. Kitts was the silence of the region from as early as the period when the no-confidence motion was being avoided.

And from the well known regional political scientist Peter Wickham:

The final major lesson here relates to the series of unusual scenarios which started with the disregard of a no-confidence vote (NCV) for well over two years and ended with an impasse where an elections supervisor walked off the job in the middle of counting and gave the Governor General "grounds" on which to delay the installation of the new Prime Minister. The last set of atrocities have been widely criticised across CARICOM, but sadly little has been said about the NCV which set the tone years before.

And from Sir Ron Sanders the prolific and well respected commentator:

In the event, what is revealed by these recent events in St Kitts-Nevis (as previously in Antigua and Barbuda when the former government illegally dismissed the Chairman and members of the Electoral Commission and attempted to change the election boundaries) is that the organisation and administration of electoral processes in a few Caribbean countries require review. It is a review that might be best carried out by all CARICOM countries collectively so as to avoid finger-pointing at any one country and the party political advantage that might be sought from it. What is at stake is the credibility and legitimacy of the electoral process throughout the Region and therefore the standing of the Caribbean itself in the eyes of foreign investors, international financial institutions, capital markets and the global community.

Don't hold your breath for any action by Caricom.

One of the activities which brings Caribbean people together, and is a unique part of Caribbean culture, is the sport of cricket. Fifteen Caribbean islands and Guyana field a common team known as the West Indies Cricket team. It is the only multi-national team that competes internationally at the highest level of any sport. By comparison each Caribbean country fields its own teams in football and athletics, the other major sports in which regional countries compete internationally. From the late 1920s when the West Indies team was established, cricket has been a major binding regional force. Our peoples were, and to a lesser extent still are, passionate about the game.

The West Indies team won the first and second Cricket World Cups in 1975 and 1979 and then absolutely dominated world cricket until 1995. Our players were heroes not only in the region but around the entire cricket world. Domination in sport is usually cyclical. Australia, India and South Africa, and to a lesser extent Sri Lanka and England, have gained pre-eminence in the past twenty years with ebbs and flows in the results and fortunes of their teams. However since 1995 the flow of West Indies cricket has been one way only and that is endlessly down. The inability to stop and reverse the flow has been due to mismanagement of the game since 2000 and the resulting failure to produce players with the pride and heart of the great players of the 1975-1995 and earlier eras. This, despite the opportunity which current players have to earn substantially from the game, a privilege which the great players prior to 1995 did not have.

The failure falls squarely at the feet of West Indies Cricket Board which administers the game in the region. Although it is in effect a public regional institution akin to Caricom and The University of the West Indies, it has been run like a private club comprising leaders of the six territorial boards who administer the game in the individual territories. While most of these people are dedicated to the game, they have lacked the management expertise, commercial skill and experience to bring West Indies cricket into the 21st century. They have guarded their turf like politicians and refused to introduce the badly needed structural changes to make the organization transparent and effective and to revive the high standards of the past. WICB competes strongly with Caricom for the title of the most dysfunctional body in the Caribbean. At time of writing WICB is virtually bankrupt with a claim for 42 million US dollars from India hanging over its head. The future of West Indies cricket is in the balance but as the saying goes the administrators 'fiddle as Rome burns'.

Appendices

I. THE FOUR SEASON ACCORD

ST. KITTS & NEVIS **CHAMBER OF INDUSTRY AND COMMERCE**

JOINT STATEMENT RESULTING FROM THE FORUM FOR NATIONAL UNITY

A Forum for National Unity was held at the Four Seasons Resort on Nevis on Tuesday, November 22, 1994.

The Forum was convened by the St. Kitts & Nevis Chamber of Industry and Commerce and was attended by representatives of the ruling PAM/NRP Coalition government, the St. Kitts-Nevis Labour Party, and the Concerned Citizens Movement of Nevis. Also in attendance were representatives of the Chamber, the Christian Councils of St. Kitts and Nevis, the Evangelical Associations of St. Kitts and Nevis, the St. Kitts-Nevis Hotel and Tourism Association, the St. Kitts-Nevis Trades and Labour Union, and the St. Kitts and Nevis Bar Association.

After extensive discussions lasting the entire day and covering all matters relevant to the present crisis facing our country the Forum for National Unity agreed that recent drug-related crime and the increase in crimes involving the use of guns pose a serious threat to the peace and security of all citizens and residents of St. Kitts and Nevis and its economy. It was particularly agreed that continued adverse publicity would erode the confidence of both local and foreign investors and could easily leave a disastrous impact on the tourism industry.

It was agreed that the following action should be taken to address these problems:

1.   Unequivocal condemnation of all drug-related criminal activity by all political parties and a joint declaration of party leaders to attack this scourge of our society. This declaration must include a public call for full co-operation with Scotland Yard's investigations and the re-assurance of the Police Force that its members will receive full support in clamping down on gun and drug-related crime in particular.

2.   Immediate review of the operations of the Police Force to improve its morale, strengthen its crime fighting capacity and to redress the current political polarisation of its Officers and ranks.

3.   Strengthening security and drug interdiction efforts at ports of entry and exit.

4.   Immediate review of Governmental and community programmes

and the development of new programmes to restore lost family, moral and civic values.

5.   Complete review of the system of appointments to Government Commissions, Boards, Corporations, Authorities and other agencies with a view to establishing greater independence and efficiency in the operation of those bodies.

6.   Strengthening the education system to counter the negative influences of the media and the drug culture.

7.   Improving local programming on the Government broadcasting service to help counter the negative influences of Cable television.

8.   General monitoring of ZIZ Radio and Television to establish a professional institution and protect its abuse for political purposes.

9.   Elimination of the use of the political party newspapers and platforms to "demonise" political opponents. The local media should be monitored by a committee comprising one nominee each of the Chamber, Christian Council, Evangelical Association, Business and Professional Womens Club, and youth groups in order to ensure compliance.

10.   Introduction of a Code of Ethics for political activity.

11.   Strengthening Government's Legal Department and the office of the Director of Public Prosecutions.

In recognition of the urgent national need for political stability while the above measures are addressed and to restore the traditional peace and stability of our islands it was agreed that this agreement should include a decision on the date for the next General Elections. It was accordingly agreed that the next General Elections be held not later than November 15, 1995. In the interim period negotiations between all political parties represented in the National Assembly will be undertaken with the view of achieving participation by all such parties in decision-making of Government relating to:
    a.   all major capital projects
    b.   all major foreign investments
    c.   land distribution
    d.   Civil Service review
    e.   Police Force improvement
    f.   Code of Conduct for political activity

The need was stressed for a "cooling off" period" in which current tensions can be allowed to dissipate. All political parties pledged to work towards this end. Specifically, there will be no public political meetings during the month of December, 1994.

The meeting was conducted in an atmosphere of utmost cordiality and mutual respect in full recognition of the importance of these deliberations to the future of our country.

SIGNED AT FOUR SEASONS RESORT, NEVIS THIS 22ND DAY OF NOVEMBER, 1994.

....
Right Honourable Dr. Kennedy A Simmonds
Prime Minister & Leader of the Peoples
Action Movement

....
Honourable Dr. Denzil Douglas
Leader of the St. Kitts-Nevis Labour Party

....
Honourable Vance Amory
Premier of Nevis & Leader of the Concerned
Citizens Movement

....
Honourable Joseph W. Parry
Leader of the Nevis Reformation Party

....
Richard O. Skerritt
President St. Kitts & Nevis Chamber of
Industry and Commerce

....
Glen Knorr
President St. Kitts-
Nevis Hotel and
Tourism Association

....
Archdeacon Rudolph Smithen
President St. Kitts Christian Council

....
Pastor Leroy Benjamin
President St. Kitts Evangelical Association

....
Reverend Joyce Rohan
for Nevis Christian Council

....
Pastor Eric Maynard
for Nevis Evangelical Association

....
Lee L. Moore, Q.C.
President St. Kitts-Nevis Trades and Labour Union

....
Charles Wilkin
President St. Kitts-Nevis Bar Association

II. PAPER ON ASPECTS OF ELECTORAL REFORM

This paper addresses the following issues relating to the electoral process. These are in our opinion the key issues to the establishment of an improved electoral process which deters and limits the abuse now commonplace.

A. Qualification for registration as a voter

B. The registration process

C. The dispute resolution process

A. QUALIFICATION FOR REGISTRATION AS A VOTER

The current law establishes as the qualifying criteria any of the following:-

1. Citizenship, age and residence in a constituency

2. Citizenship, age and domicile in a constituency

3. Commonwealth citizenship, age and residence in the Federation for 12 months or domicile and residence in the Federation at the date of registration

1 is hereafter referred to as the 'residence qualification'

2 is hereafter to as the 'domicile qualification' or 'the overseas voter qualification.'

3 is hereafter referred to as the 'Commonwealth citizenship qualification.'

1. RESIDENCE QUALIFICATION

Ordinary residence of a person is defined in the current law as "generally that place which has always been, or which he has adopted as, the place of his habitation or home, whereof when away from there he intends to return." That definition leaves the question to the subjective determination of the applicant for registration. There are a myriad of scenarios which we could outline to show how this definition can be abused and everyone agrees that it has been abused. Residence is a question of fact to be determined not only on the intention of the voter but on actual existing factual circumstances.

While therefore the definition must of necessity be general the rules governing the registration process must be tight enough to produce a proper determination of the question.

We recommend the Antigua provision in respect of 'ordinary residence' which is "Any question as to a person's residence on the dates for application for registration shall be determined in accordance with the general principles applied in determining questions as to a person's residence and, in particular, regard shall be had to the purpose and other circumstances, as well as to the fact, of his presence at, or absence from the address in question."

2. DOMICILE QUALIFICATION

The domicile qualification was introduced by the 1983 amendment to the electoral law. Regulation 6 of the Election Registration Regulations 1984 (SRO No. 5 of 1984) states that for purposes of registration, domicile means domicile of origin or domicile of choice. These are complex legal concepts and result in the expressions "ordinary residence" and "domicile" not being synonymous.

A domicile of origin is attributed to all persons at birth by operation of law and (in St. Kitts-Nevis where illegitimacy has been legally abolished) is the domicile of one's father, or of one's mother if one's father is deceased at birth.

After attaining adulthood, every person is free to acquire a domicile of choice in substitution for that which he/she possessed immediately prior to such choice. There is no limit to the number of times a person may change their domicile of choice. Domicile of choice is acquired, and can be changed, by a person actually taking up residence at a particular place, coupled with the intention to live there permanently. Once there is the simultaneous existence of residence and intention to permanently remain, the law does not require such factual residence to be for any particular period. In addition, temporary absences from the address of one's domicile of choice would not result in loss of one's domicile of choice.

It will therefore be appreciated that use of the concepts of domicile of origin and domicile of choice as qualifying persons for registration to vote result in the franchise or right to vote being no longer rooted in residence.

The continued retention of these domicile concepts or principles in our electoral law will perpetuate precisely the mischief and "serious consequences" which the late Sir Lee L Moore Q.C. argued against as described in the The Labour Spokesman editorial of 2nd November 1983. Continued use of the domicile qualification in our electoral law would have the undesirable effects described by Sir Lee L Moore QC in 1983:

- "... the people living in St. Kitts-Nevis could find their wishes overruled by people living abroad."

- "... subvert democracy, making the exercise of the franchise of no effect and giving rise to instability in the country."

As Mr Moore put it: there are "differences between citizenship and the franchise, citizenship being concerned with allegiance and protection, the franchise being related to place of residence", (Labour Spokesman editorial, 2 November 1983).

From his quoted comments in The Labour Spokesman, it is clear that Mr Moore expected that the changes made to the 1983 amending Act would have preserved actual residence as being a requirement for voter registration. The final wording of the 1983 amendment, coupled with the wording in the Election Registration Regulations, 1984 (see Regulations 5 and 6) frustrated such expectation and undermined fundamental principles. It is necessary to examine the fundamental principles as they relate to this issue.

Domicile was, and continues to be, an inappropriate criterion for registration as a voter because of the tenuous connection with St. Kitts-Nevis, far less any particular constituency, that it requires. This weakness of connection is further exacerbated by Regulation 6 which appears to permit one to rely upon either domicile of origin or domicile of choice.

The concept of domicile is principally used in law to determine which territory's laws apply to regulate an individual's personal status, applicable inheritance rules and such like. For these purposes, under the general (ie. non-electoral) law:-

1. Nobody shall be without a domicile.

2. A person cannot have two domiciles. Domicile signifies connection with what has conveniently been called a "law district", ie. a territory subject to a single system of law.

We strongly recommend that the overseas voter qualification be abolished and that qualification be restricted to the residence qualification and the Commonwealth citizenship qualification. If however it is felt that the horse has already bolted the awful concept of domicile should be replaced by allowing citizens of St. Kitts-Nevis resident abroad to register in a constituency with which they have a 'real connection' such as place of birth (which can be verified from a birth certificate) or the last place of residence in St. Kitts-Nevis for more than 12 months as verifiable by documentary proof as in the case of the residence qualification. In addition, such residence should be verified by an affidavit of a person resident in St. Kitts-Nevis and on the voters list for that constituency. The questionnaire attached as Appendix A can be modified to suit this form of application. The applicant should himself/herself also swear an affidavit as to the truth of his/her answers to the questionnaire.

B. THE REGISTRATION PROCESS

In his judgment in the Lindsay Grant election petition Mr Justice Belle said at paragraph 57 "After listening to the submissions of counsel, reviewing the law and the various factual accounts, I am convinced that the process of registration of voters in St. Kitts and Nevis is seriously flawed. Indeed when a person registers as a voter to have their name placed on a voters list there appears to be no request for evidence of identity." In our opinion the current regulations governing the process are lax and totally unsatisfactory. The registration officer is given wide latitude including the power to determine whether or not to ask for any supporting documents as to the residence or domicile of an applicant or whether to require the applicant to make a statutory declaration to support his claim. The absence of documentary evidence makes an absurdity of the review process, especially as the first adjudicator of claims and objections is the registration officer himself. Not only is there an appeal to Caesar from Caesar but there are no rules governing either stage of the process. This process is tailor-made for abuse.

We make the following recommendations to be included in new regulations:

1. There should be a standard questionnaire which each applicant claiming a residence qualification must complete at the registration office. An applicant should be allowed to bring with him/her one person to assist in completing the questionnaire. The questionnaire would impose a standard for all applicants. A model questionnaire is attached as Appendix A.

   The purpose of questions 12 to 16 on Appendix A is to provide a deterrent to false statements of the applicant's address in 4. If he states an address in 4 but answers no to question 12 he could be exposed to a perjury charge if it is proven on objection that he does spend more than [36] hours per week at an address other than that in 4. It will also enable the registration officer to determine which of 2 addresses is the ordinary residence of an applicant who genuinely spends substantial time at more than one address.

2. The applicant should verify the truth of his/her answers to the questionnaire by an oath taken before the registration officer. Registration officers

should for the purpose be made Commissioners for Oaths. This would be an incentive for accurate information to be provided with the deterrent of a charge of perjury for any applicant who lies in his answers to the questionnaire.

3. Each applicant should produce the following documents to the registration officer who should make copies of them for the applicant's file:

a) Passport

b) Driver's licence

c) Latest utility bills for electricity, water, cable tv and fixed line telephone.

If the applicant does not produce any of these documents the registration officer should record that fact on the file and any reason proferred by the applicant for not having these documents. If he pays for utilities supplied to more than one address he should disclose this fact.

4. The registration officer should create a file for each applicant with the completed questionnaire and all supporting documents. The registration officer should write his determination of the application on a standard form. He should state his reasons if he refuses the application.

5. The file should be available to any person who pays a search fee of $10. Fees collected in this way would assist in meeting the costs of the process.

6. In the event of an objection being made to the qualification of the applicant the person objecting should have the right to apply to the Court for an order requiring the Passport Office, the Social Security Board, or any of the utility providers to produce its records relating to the address of the applicant and if there are none, to so state.

The registration process should take place entirely within the Federation. Our reasons for this proposal are cost considerations for the public purse, transparency and public confidence.

C. THE DISPUTE RESOLUTION PROCESS

Disputes arise in one of two ways:

1. An applicant is refused registration by the registration officer and challenges that decision.

2. Any third party objects to the registration of the applicant.

   Because of the standard and more thorough registration process than presently applies there should be no need for the registration officer to hear claims and objections. These should go directly to the High Court. The Judge should conduct a full hearing on the facts and law and should have available the file made by the registration officer and any affidavits filed and written submissions made by the parties to the claim or objection.

The parties should appear before the Court in person and should have the right to Counsel, to call or subpoena witnesses and to cross examine the other party and his witnesses. Evidence in chief should be provided by way of affidavit. The parties should also file written submissions. These requirements would reduce the time taken by the Court to hear each claim or objection. The current rules of the High Court contain a workable process to facilitate speedy hearings of claims and objections via fixed date claim forms.

3. There should be an appeal to the Court of Appeal on a point of law only.

   In the event of a re-registration for the completion of a new voters list the Government should request that the Chief Justice assign a High Court judge to sit exclusively for the hearing of claims and objections. This would facilitate the speedy resolution of disputes.

   In this event also the period for filing claims and objections should be at least 30 days after initial publication of the list. Once a list is established the period for filing claims and objections can be reduced.

....

CHARLES WILKIN, Q.C.

....

J EMILE FERDINAND

21 August 2007

QUESTIONNAIRE

(Residence Qualification)

1. Full Name of applicant:...

2. Age of applicant: ....

3. Citizenship(s) held by applicant:...

4. Address of residence of applicant:..

5. How long have you lived at that address: ....

6. Do you own the property/apartment/room at that address:

....

7. Do you rent the property/apartment/room at that address: ....

8. If you do not own or rent, with whose permission do you occupy the property/apartment/room:

....

9. What is your relationship to that person: ....

10. Do you pay for any of the following utilities provided to your above address - √ or X as applicable.

    Electricity -   ☐

    Water -   ☐

    Cable TV -   ☐

    Fixed line telephone - ☐

11. Are you registered with the Social Security Board? .... If so, what is youraddress as provided to the Social Security Board?

....

12. Do you have a valid St Kitts-Nevis Passport? .... If so, what is the number? ....

13. Do you spend more than [36] hours per week at any other address. If so, state that address:

....

14. Do you own or rent the property/apartment/room at that address?

....

15. If not, with whose permission do you stay at that address: ....

....

16. What is your relationship to that person? ....

17. Do you pay for any of the following utilities provided to that address:

    Electricity -   ☐

    Water -   ☐

    Cable TV -   ☐

    Fixed line telephone -   ☐

I _____ do solemnly swear that all answers
         Name of Applicant

and information provided by me in the above questionnaire are true and correct and that I have not withheld or failed to disclose any information in answer to any of the above questions.

WARNING: Applicants are warned that any false answers and/or information included on this questionnaire can result in CRIMINAL PROSECUTION and the imposition of severe penalties, including fines and/or imprisonment.

Sworn by   ) ....

at   )   Signature of Applicant

this day of 2007   )

Before me:

....

Commissioner for Oaths

ST. KITTS AND NEVIS NATIONAL COMPETITIVENESS COUNCIL

REPORT

September 30, 2010

PREFACE

The National Competitiveness Council (the "Council") was established on 22nd December 2009 as part of the Government's Private Sector Development Strategy, and began work in late January 2010.

A list of its members appears on page 4.

The terms of reference of the Council are set out on pages 5-6.

It is to be noted that the remit of the Council is purely advisory. It is to be expected however that serious consideration will be given by the Government to recommendations of the Council. The Council has to date received full and excellent support from all officials, agencies and departments of Government with which it has interacted.

The terms of reference are very wide and require the Council to review the whole economic and social framework of the country. The terms require the Council to issue an annual report.

Despite its relatively short existence the Council has decided to issue its first report at this time because, in its assessment, some of its recommendations require urgent action and have budgetary implications.

At the outset the Council decided to establish an Objective Statement containing the measurable objectives which it suggests for economic development. The deliberations of the Council should focus on recommendations to achieve the stated objectives. The Objective Statement begins on page 7.

The Council has discussed a wide range of issues affecting the competitiveness of the country and its economic and social development but it has decided to focus this first report on issues affecting the preparedness of our human resources to compete internationally and for the country to improve its business climate. These issues are reported under the following headings:

1. Human Resources and Related Issues, and

2. The Business Climate and Entrepreneurship.

Other issues of relevance will be addressed in later reports, including the state of the major industries outlined in the Objective Statement, public sector reform, a detailed look at training and the pros and cons of increasing the size of the population as a means of expanding the economy.

Another issue which the Council has considered and which presents enormous challenges is the issue of violent crime. This phenomenon has the potential to decimate the economy. Beginning at page 26 is a resolution passed by the Council on 27th May 2010 and sent immediately to the Prime Minister. The Council cannot overstate the seriousness of this threat.

As is recognized in the report competitiveness is a journey not a destination. Success for St Kitts and Nevis on that journey will be heavily dependant on substantial economic and social changes including increased fiscal discipline at the national level, excellence in the service industries, quality in manufacturing and improved productivity throughout the public and private sectors. The entire society must establish and maintain an awareness to improve its social discipline as a basis for the changes required to achieve international competitiveness.

St. Kitts-Nevis are, to repeat the true and well worn phrase, at the crossroads. To produce positive results the application of fiscal discipline must be accompanied by fundamental changes in the mindset, attitudes, politics and culture of our people. Unless these changes are made we face the risk, as a nation, of retrogressing. Our report contains substantial recommendations in this regard.

In his address at the official ceremony to mark the 25th Anniversary of Independence in 2008 the Honourable Prime Minister said that an improvement in attitudes is key to the development of St. Kitts and Nevis in the next 25 years. We wholeheartedly endorse that sentiment and call on our society not to delay in planning in a unified manner the action necessary to reverse the negative attitudes which have pervaded our culture.

We thank the Prime Minister and his Cabinet for the confidence placed by them in our ability to make a difference through our work. We will do all within our power to contribute meaningfully to the development of St. Kitts and Nevis.

INDEX

NATIONAL COMPETITIVENESS COUNCIL

LIST OF MEMBERS

Charles L. A. Wilkin, CMG, QC, MA (Cantab) (Chairman)	Senior Partner, Kelsick, Wilkin & Ferdinand
Ernest Amory, MBE.	Partner, Amory Enterprises
Keisha Archibald, BSc.	IT Projects Co-ordinator
Scott R. Caines, BA, CPA.	Chairman, C & C Group of Companies
Kishu D. Chandiramani, MBE	Chairman, Rams Group of Companies
Dr. Simon Jones-Hendrickson, Ph.D.	Professor of Economics, University of the Virgin Islands
Earle A. Kelly, BA, MBA.	Executive Director, TDC Group of Companies
W. Anthony Kelsick, BA, B.Comm, CA	Chairman, Horsfords Group of Companies
Sir Edmund W. Lawrence, KCMG, OBE, CSM, JP	Managing Director, National Bank Group of Companies
Wendell E. Lawrence, BSc., CPA	Financial Consultant
Dr. Osbert W. Liburd, Ph.D.	Biologist and Plant Pathologist
Judith Rawlins	Designer/Manager, Brown Sugar

TERMS OF REFERENCE

NAME
The National Competitiveness Council of Advisers.

THE MISSION
The National Competitiveness Council of Advisers shall conduct research, brainstorm on key social and economic issues affecting the Federation of St. Kitts and Nevis, and provide policy advice and recommendations to the Prime Minister with a view to enhancing the competitiveness of St. Kitts and Nevis; strengthening the economic climate and legal framework to make it more conducive to entrepreneurship, business development, and investment; and fostering income generation, employment creation, economic growth and the overall economic and social development of St. Kitts and Nevis.

TERMS OF REFERENCE
The Council will do all that is necessary to carry out its Mission including the following activities:-

❖ Provide policy advice and/or recommendations to the Prime Minister on matters referred to The Council by the Prime Minister from time to time, and on an ongoing basis on all matters relating to the Mission of The Council.

❖ Identify on an ongoing basis legal and administrative impediments to business development and to the implementation of policies relevant to the Mission of The Council and recommend appropriate changes that would improve the business climate and facilitate the implementation of policies relating to business development, local and foreign investment, and the enhancement of competitiveness.

❖ Conduct research in any area deemed by The Council to be of relevance to its Mission and likely to result in findings that would contribute to the quality of its policy advice and/or recommendations to the Prime Minister or to the efficacy of economic decision-making by the Government.

❖ Liaise with other Government decision-making bodies engaged in activities related to the Mission of the Council with a view to ensuring a coordinated approach in respect of the relevant policy initiatives pursued by the Government.

❖ Consult with private sector entities and Non-Governmental Organizations from time to time when, in the opinion of The Council, the policy advice and/or recommendations to be provided to the Prime Minister or otherwise in fulfilment of the Mission would be significantly enhanced by such consultation and would ensure that appropriate weight is given to the views, concerns and interests of stakeholders likely to be affected by the relevant policies.

❖ Carry out the role, functions and mandate of the Competitiveness Council proposed in the Government's Private Sector Development Strategy that was funded by the European Union.

❖ Produce and publish a report on an annual basis outlining the recommendations made by it over the prior year and the rationale for same.

STRUCTURE, COMPOSITION AND OPERATIONS

The members of The Council (including a Chairman) shall be appointed by the Prime Minister, and shall possess among them, the range of skills experience and expertise required for the effective discharge of the functions of the Council.

The Council shall have at least nine (9) members and no more that twelve (12) members.

The Council shall be provided a Secretariat with access to appropriate consultancy, technical and administrative services to effectively support the work of the Council and to carry out on behalf of the Council such research and analysis as is necessary from time to time in keeping with the Mission of the Council.

OBJECTIVE STATEMENT

"To facilitate, through the execution of its mandate, the creation of a strong and internationally competitive service-based economy with excellent service in every sector, vibrant entrepreneurship, a productive and motivated human resource base and a good quality of life for all."

Key Sectors

The following sectors have been identified as the pillars on which the service-based economy should be built:

> ➢ Tourism
> ➢ Offshore University Services
> ➢ Information and Communication Technologies
> ➢ Financial Services
> ➢ Manufacturing with special emphasis on food processing, cottage industries, niche products and other high value added products

Support Sectors

The following supporting sectors may complement the key sectors identified above, by fostering economic activity in the various communities and/or by supplying goods and services to the key sectors and minimizing the leakages from the foreign exchange inflows emanating from the export of the output of the key sectors:-

> ➢ Agriculture
> ➢ Handicraft
> ➢ Retail and Commerce

Key Areas of Focus

> ➢ Human Resource Development
>
> ➢ Doing Business Survey
>   - Government Systems and Processes
>   - Professional Services (including appropriate regulation and ethical standards)
>   - Public Sector Reform
>
> ➢ Public Education

> ➢ Economic climate, including tax policy, fiscal performance, debt management, balance of payments, economic growth and other key indicators of macro-economic stability.

> ➢ Social Development, including poverty reduction

> ➢ Protection of the Environment

> ➢ Constitutional, Legal and Regulatory issues

> ➢ Foster entrepreneurship (including small business development and financing)

> ➢ Enterprise financing including capital market development

> ➢ Investment Promotion and Facilitation (domestic and foreign)

> ➢ Technological Development

> ➢ Intellectual Property

> ➢ Safety and Security

> ➢ Government Services

> ➢ International profile and image, including presence in International Institutions and informal interaction and networking

> ➢ The role of nationals overseas

These areas are cross cutting in that the work of the Council in any of these areas is likely to affect most or all of the key and supporting sectors identified. They would therefore complement the sector-specific initiatives of the Council. While the mandate of the Council is primarily advisory, the Council may also wish to indicate areas where, based on the expertise of members, a more hands-on approach would be appropriate. This would then permit the Council, in its reports, to offer its more direct assistance in specific areas.

REPORT OF NATIONAL COMPETITIVENESS COUNCIL

NOTION OF COMPETITIVENESS

We begin with some comments on the notion of competitiveness. According to the World Economic Forum's "The Global Competitive Report", a country is characterized as competitive if it provides high levels of prosperity to its people. In turn this is a function of how productively the country uses its available resources. The World Economic Forum, which has been at the forefront of national competitiveness analysis for three decades, has adopted a global competitiveness index comprising 12 of what it calls pillars by which it assesses the competitiveness of individual countries. The IDB has recently applied these pillars in its assessment of the competitiveness of 5 Caricom countries-Barbados, Guyana, Jamaica, Trinidad and Tobago and Suriname. As far as we are aware no international body has carried out such formal assessment of St. Kitts and Nevis. The Council does not presently have the data and research support that would enable us to carry out ourselves an assessment of that type.

We note that competitiveness can be an elusive concept and the traditional pillars or variables may be useful but not entirely sufficient for a true evaluation of our situation. Competitiveness is not static, it is a dynamic process. We have in our short existence sought to identify and analyze some of the pillars or variables which we consider of immediate relevance to us. Our first report will focus on human resource issues and the business climate.

GENERAL OBSERVATIONS

Before we get more specific we make a few general points:-

1. The size of our country should not be a deterrent to its competing globally. Despite being one of the smallest nations in the world in terms of physical size and population, St. Kitts and Nevis has achieved a standard of living and a quality of life in excess of many larger, developing nations. We should not therefore approach our development with the negative attitude that our small size prevents us from competing.

2. No country in the world is competitive in all industries. A country can be globally competitive only in a few industries. China dominates in export manufacturing, Japan in electronics, the USA in the IT industry and Barbados in tourism. It is critical in our approach to become globally competitive that we decide definitively the industries and sub-sectors of industries in which we will seek to be competitive. We will revert to this point later.

3. We must first define ourselves as a country in order to define our path to competitiveness.

4. The Council supports the view strongly promoted by Professor Michael Porter, the guru in this field of economics, that productivity sets a nation's standard of living and is therefore a key factor in determining how competitive a country will be.

5. We take the view that the economy of St. Kitts and Nevis is at the crossroads. The factors which will propel it positively forward are a careful selection of the industries in which it will seek to compete, improved productivity at every level and in every such industry, the development of a culture of excellence in service (of which we are quite capable) and a cohesive approach to our development involving all sectors of our society using the maximum brain power available to plan and innovate.

6. The major threats to our development are, in our opinion, low levels of productivity and efficiency, unacceptably high level of crime, the high national debt, the political polarization and disunity of our society and the generally declining attitudes and ill discipline.

7. In the development of selected industries and in all commercial and public enterprises we must promote and factor in the use of cutting edge technology to improve our competitiveness.

We turn now to the specific recommendations.

INDUSTRY SELECTION

We noted earlier that a critical component in competitiveness is the correct selection of industries on which the country should focus. Tourism is currently our major industry. We do not believe that the country will be able to compete in mass tourism. We support instead the pursuit of up market tourism and niche areas such as medical tourism, sports tourism, ecumenical tourism, convention tourism and education tourism.

The Council is of the view that our greatest strength is in offshore education services which sector brings benefits in both education and tourism. It is our strongly held view that we can and should seek to become a world leader in this field. This industry already contributes about 10-12 per cent of our GDP and, despite the world economic recession, continues to grow. If the projections in the near term increase in total numbers of students to 3,500 materializes it may well surpass tourism as the largest contributor to GDP. Its orderly growth should be dynamically pursued. We cannot but note that Government spends millions, as it should, on tourism promotion but there isn't a single Government office devoted to the promotion of the offshore education sector. We should not take that industry for granted. We must build on the strong competitive advantage which we presently hold. We have read carefully the ISSED report entitled "Strategy and Action Plan for the Offshore Education Sector". We support the call in that document for Government to build its institutional support for the sector, including the strengthening of the Accreditation Board and greater standardization and transparency in the investment process.

We recommend that Government convene a conference involving the industry and civil society to review that report and to place the development of that key industry on the front burner.

Stronger marketing and public relations support is also required for the sector. The need to minimize threats to the security of this sector must be ascribed high priority.

There is also a planning aspect to the further development of this sector. Thought should be given to the creation of clusters around the offshore schools to exploit the economic synergies.

Manufacturing, particularly in the area of electronics assembly, continues to be a major contributor in terms of employment and exports. While we are cognizant of the threats to that sector we urge Government to nurture it as best it can.

We do not see a great future for the financial services industry in its present form, at least not in St. Kitts. We recommend that the current model be reviewed. We do not know enough about Nevis' latest thrust in that industry to comment on it or to learn from it for the entire Federation.

HUMAN RESOURCES AND RELATED ISSUES

As the economy will be dependent primarily on service industries the development of our human resources will be key to St. Kitts and Nevis in its bid to become internationally competitive. There are currently several deficiencies in this area.

SERVICE

To compete strongly we must improve our levels of service. The pursuit of excellence in service should be a major plank in the further development of our service-oriented economy. The aim should be to create as part of our culture, without losing any of the other positive aspects, a commitment to and pride in excellent service. We cannot rely simply on our friendliness and warmth as a people. Excellent service should complement our natural friendliness and warmth. Likewise, excellence in the delivery of service should become part of our national identity. With the correct social and economic stimulation that is an achievable goal over the medium term.

There has been insufficient emphasis on the quality of service in our tourism product and generally. There has not been a continuous and concerted national effort to promote the ideals of excellent service and to sensitize the public to its importance to the livelihood of everyone. Such effort is now essential. We set out what we perceive as the broad parameters of such effort:

1. It should include the establishment with public/private sector consensus of standards of excellence in each industry and sector and a system to measure and report on the quality of service in the key economic sectors. There are ample precedents from work done by other countries which we can study and adopt or adapt to our needs.

2. It should include a massive public awareness campaign with a positive message of empowerment and focus on the importance of excellent service and positive attitudes towards self, work and country.

3. It should inculcate an intolerance for poor service and encourage everyone to demand excellent service.

4. It should target negative attitudes which militate against good service such as:-

    a) the confusion of service with servitude.

    b) the increasing hostility in inter-personal relations and contact within our community; and

    c) negative attitudes which contribute to ill-discipline and disorder in the society.

5. It should include a message of the importance of productivity to economic development as outlined below.

6. The messages should be embedded in the school curriculum at every level and brought to public attention by the most effective means of communication.

7. The campaign should be spread initially over 2-3 years with provision for extension if necessary.

8. Pre-qualified locally owned entities, and joint ventures including local entities, with experience and expertise in this area, should be invited on a competitive basis to submit their recommended public awareness campaign and bid for executing same.

9. We are not experts in this field but the campaign should include the following:-

   a) a slogan competition with substantial prizes;

   b) highlighting of exemplary individuals and businesses;

   c) the use of vehicle licence plates to carry a suitable slogan;

   d) radio and tv advertising sponsored by local businesses; and

   e) billboards and other effective promotional methods.

10. An initial budget should be established of EC$100,000 to meet the cost of the campaign.

11. An organizing committee should be established and provided with the budget to arrange and oversee the campaign.

12. Representatives of the media should be included in that committee as media houses should play a key role in implementation of the campaign and will benefit from it.

13. The National Competitiveness Council is prepared to participate in the organizing committee.

PRODUCTIVITY

There is an inextricable link between productivity and prosperity. Productivity growth in the private sector tends to lead to increased profits which benefit shareholders, employees and consumers and increase Government tax revenue. Productivity growth in the public sector tends to lead to cost efficiencies and savings to the public purse and contributes to productivity in the private sector. Strong national productivity makes a country more competitive and attractive to local and foreign investors.

"Over long periods of time, small differences in rates of productivity growth compound, like interest in a bank account, and can make an enormous difference to a society's prosperity. Nothing contributes more to material well-being, to the reduction of poverty, to increases in leisure time, and to a country's ability to finance education, public health, environment and the arts than its productivity growth rate" (Baumol, Williams J and Alan S. Blinder 2009, 11th Edition 491).

This message needs to be adequately communicated in St. Kitts-Nevis. Sustained increases in productivity should become a national goal and should be strongly but simply communicated as such.

We recommend a review of best international practices in this area and the adoption of a system to assess and measure productivity in all sectors

DISCIPLINE AND ORDER

These are key ingredients in the image and development of any country. Ill-discipline and disorder are too prevalent in our community and are growing alarmingly. They negatively affect the standards of service and productivity and should be confronted simultaneously with the pursuit of excellence in service. Many of the laws which provide the foundation for such confrontation already exist. We recommend that they be more stringently enforced, including the laws against littering, loitering, noise pollution and illegal vending. The blocking of sidewalks and lack of respect for traffic laws, which create disorder on the roads of Basseterre in particular, should also be confronted by additional legislation where necessary (e.g to establish bus stops) and enforcement of these and existing laws should be stepped up.

By way of example an experienced observer noted over the period of five minutes on a busy lunch hour between the Circus and Bay Road 16 open and flagrant infractions of the law. While this is not a scientific sample it points to an anecdotal case to which attention should be paid and appropriate action taken.

Harassment of visitors in Basseterre and on the beaches is also growing and must be addressed now before it escalates beyond reasonable control.

BEAUTIFICATION

The appearance and cleanliness of a country go hand in hand with service in the attraction of visitors and investment. St. Kitts has outstanding beauty and has always had a good reputation for cleanliness of its public areas. This reputation is being eroded. A positive effort should be made to reverse the decline and to enhance the beauty of Basseterre and the countryside. To this end we recommend:

1. The creation of an Historic Basseterre zone by legislation which controls building design and standards in the zone and includes incentives for maintenance and reconstruction of buildings within the zone.

2. The Basseterre Beautiful Committee should be reactivated with participation of private and public sector representatives. This committee should be given statutory status in the legislation referred to above and be given responsibility for

planning the enhancement of the historic zone including Independence Square and The Circus.

3. A similar committee should be established for planning the beautification of the villages and countryside. This committee should include "elders" and youth of the rural communities.

4. Legislation should be enforced (and amended where necessary) to compel the owners of vacant lots throughout the nation to keep them clean. Government should be empowered to contract for the cleaning of lots which are not kept clean by the owner and Government should levy a charge onto the property tax of the owner to cover the cost. This will help from several perspectives by removing a haven for vermin, contributing to the clean appearance of the islands and provide work for cleaning contractors and personnel. Current efforts in this regard are not effective.

5. The unsightly and chaotic Basseterre bus terminal should be cleaned up, reorganised and improved.

6. A careful and comprehensive look should be taken at the planning of the greater Basseterre area.

TRAFFIC IN AND AROUND BASSETERRE

Ease of movement is important to visitors who do not want to spend long periods in traffic, particularly on a small island. This is becoming more frequently the case in St. Kitts. We recommend that a general review be undertaken with public consultation on the traffic system in Basseterre with a view to reducing congestion. To improve traffic flows in the capital consideration should be given to increasing the number of roads restricted to one way traffic.

Consideration should also be given to establishing minimum speed limits on the Frigate Bay Road, the Sir Kennedy Simmonds Highway and the F.T Williams By pass road. We do not advocate speeding but these are our equivalent of highways and it is not unusual to have minimum speed limits on highways. Motorists should not have the frustration and danger of driving on these roads behind cars which are crawling for leisure or for whatever other reason.

The use of the highways by learner drivers should not be permitted during the morning and afternoon "rush hours".

PUBLIC SECTOR REFORM

We view the proposed public sector reform as important in the thrust for excellent service nationally and for improved productivity. We welcome its immediacy as expressed in the Throne Speech at the recent opening of the current National Assembly. We trust that it will effectively modernize the public service. We urge that a measurable improvement in the standard of public service be forged by a streamlined structure and enforced efficiencies. An essential ingredient of the reform must be training which emphasizes a too often overlooked fact that Civil Servants are appointed to serve. Civil Servants should be made to understand that the taxes of residents pay their salaries. We expect also that the reform will establish new standards for recruitment of Civil Servants, for assessing their performance, for determining the award of contracts and other Government services and a new openness in Government processes. We look forward to participating in the debate on this subject.

TRAINING

The importance of training cannot be overstated. As indicated above we get the clear impression that the levels of training within our key sectors are variable and sporadic.

While it is not possible to compel or to standardize training we feel that it should be possible to sensitize the participants to the importance of training. This should be done by consultation between the private and public sector agencies in each industry and particularly in tourism.

At an institutional level we support the policy of upgrading the CFB College to a University. In terms of education for tourism a careful review is required of the training offered at the CFB Tourism and Hospitality school. That school should be upgraded in consultation with and involvement of the industry.

Potential co-operation with the offshore schools should be explored.

Particular attention should be paid to technical/vocational and service training and to training geared to producing entrepreneurs.

We are aware of the Education White Paper and research and review being undertaken in this area and look forward to the product of such exercises. We recommend this as an area for more in depth study by this Council in 2011.

POLITICAL CULTURE
The political culture on St. Kitts clearly impacts negatively upon productivity in our economy and therefore our competitiveness. The extraordinary depth of

political rivalries and the widely held perception that progress is dependent on party affiliation have led to an unhealthy divide. This has engrained in too many of our people the attitude that if they are supporters of the party in power they need not be productive and if they are supporters of the party in opposition they should not be productive. Many Government supporters assume that they are entitled to advantage and many opposition supporters assume that they will be disadvantaged. Neither is necessarily the case but perception is often more powerful than reality. In this case any such perception should be reversed. Party above all else should become Country above Self or at the very least Country and Self. The political tribalism from which we suffer will not easily be changed but its continuance will severely harm the continued conversion of our economy and efforts to improve our competitiveness. We suggest the following measures to address this issue:

1 Public sector reform should make the Government recruitment, procurement and contract award processes more open

2. Consideration should be given to the introduction of Freedom of Information legislation.

3. Representatives and Senators should (by their language and conduct) show greater respect for each other in National Assembly proceedings.

4. Politicians should (by their language and conduct) show greater respect for each other generally and encourage their supporters to do likewise.

5. The services of ZIZ should be improved to make the station a truly national one accessible to all views as was agreed in the Four Seasons Accord of 1994.

6. Representatives of all political parties should be invited to participate in broad based discussions with Government and the social partners on issues of national importance such as crime, public sector reform and tax reform. Excessive politicization of these issues is harmful.

7. The Prime Minister should initiate the action above and other action to unify the country.

8. As a tangible sign of such intent all party political signage remaining in place from the 2010 General Election should be removed. The law should require all political signage to be removed from public display three weeks after elections are concluded.

EMPLOYER/EMPLOYEE RELATIONS

We are aware of the importance of good employer/employee relations to service excellence and productivity and thereby to competitiveness of the country. We think it is a fair assessment that such relations are generally good and that the current system in St. Kitts and Nevis, based on consultation through the tri-partite process and dispute resolution through conciliation, has worked.

We accept that the system can always be improved but we warn against wholesale changes. We particularly warn against legislative action to "entrench" employment as has been done in some neighbouring countries. Such action may well be counterproductive and discourage investment in labour intensive enterprise

Significant changes to the system should be made only on the basis of tripartite consensus

BUSINESS CLIMATE AND ENTREPRENEURSHIP

The economic reality is that the private sector is the engine of growth and that Government's primary role (rather than being a direct participant in business) should be as facilitator of that growth and beneficiary of taxes resulting therefrom to fund its programmes and operations.

The measures recommended are intended to enhance Government's facilitation of the private sector and its promotion of investment, both local and foreign. The measures recommended will also remove some existing disincentives to investment and to doing business generally.

TAXATION

1. The rate of corporate income tax of 35 per cent is comparatively high. Despite the difficult economic times this rate should be kept under constant review. Reduction of the rate will stimulate additional local investment which should more than offset the taxation revenue lost directly as a consequence of the reduction.

2. The entire system of corporate taxation should be reviewed with a view to removing several anomalies which are unique in the OECS, unfairly tax capital and retard business start ups and investment. These include restrictions on capital allowances, losses carried forward, group tax relief, deductible earnings and on depreciation of buildings constructed before 1996.

3. There have been substantial improvements in recent years in the collection of Government revenue by the Inland Revenue Department and Customs. There is still however not a fully level playing field. This is a major disincentive to business. Taxes should be collected across the board without fear or favour. Current abuses and weaknesses include under collection on persons making shopping trips to Statia and St. Maarten, under invoicing, favoritism and failure to collect at point of entry. We recommend that further improvements be made in the resources of the Inland Revenue Department and Customs and in their collection efforts.

4. The Ministry of Finance is not sure of the total tax base because many businesses fall between the cracks and are not registered or pay taxes. This includes some of the informal trading sector and many services. The introduction of VAT may not necessarily improve this situation. Improved identification of businesses liable to tax and collection from such businesses is essential to level the playing field and to increase Government revenues.

VAT

It is understood that the implementation of VAT in St Kitts and Nevis is being done to bring us in line with other countries in the region and in fact the world as well as to capture the potential tax revenues from the consumption of services which are currently not being taxed or taxed at a rate lower than the consumption of goods.

There are areas of concern or caution however which the Council feels ought to be noted in the implementation of VAT, namely:

Implementation issues. While there will be several issues to be dealt with at the time of implementation, one of the more pressing ones is the matter of existing goods and inventories which will be on hand at that time. Unless a proper approach is applied there is a great risk of one or all of the following: a double taxation on those goods, an immediate significant increase in the cost of these goods to the final consumer and/or a significant loss of profit to the merchant.

Tax Rate. A rate of 17% has been established. This is 1 to 2 % points more than the rates in other OECS economies. Based on experience of other OECS economies, VAT could increase tax revenues by $45 million to $80 million. Most of the increase in revenues will come from VAT on services. This tax on services will be borne almost entirely by the consumer as businesses will have the ability to apply these increased VAT tax expenses from services (input vat) against VAT payable from sales(output vat).

VAT will also have the effect of increasing the cost of goods to the consumer. For goods which currently bear the full consumption tax rate of 22.5 %, VAT will exceed this tax which it will replace by 25-30 % and the likely cost of these goods to the consumer by over 3%. For the basket of basic foods on which the consumption tax is zero, VAT may increase the cost of these goods by 17%.VAT will therefore result in significant inflation in goods and more so in food. VAT on goods could increase tax revenues by $20- $30 million.

Added to the more significant increased cost of services, the cost of living to the consumer may increase significantly, which will have the unintended effect of contracting the economy to an extent to threaten the desired increase in tax revenues. The Council is recommending that this be monitored carefully to get the accurate economic and statistical impact.

The lower income consumer will bear an undue proportion of the tax burden as several of the existing zero consumption tax basic food items have not been given the same zero rating under VAT. This sector spends a higher proportion of their disposable income on these basic food items than other sectors do. Therefore the impact on the cost of living may be greater for this sector than any other unless some consideration is given to their stitution.

FISCAL INCENTIVES

Fiscal incentives are an important means of encouraging investment in targeted sectors and in promoting economic development. The grant of such incentives should however be fully regulated.

We note that, quite properly, statutory authority was obtained by way of the St. Christopher and Nevis (Special Resort Development) Act 2007 for incentives to Christophe Harbour and any other real estate developments to come of more than 350 acres. Many other fiscal incentives are however granted without statutory authority or in excess of the limits of such authority where legislation exists.

We note that the Fiscal Incentives Act which provided the statutory basis for incentives to manufacturers was passed into law in 1974. The Hotels Aid Act which governs incentives to hotels was passed in 1956. Neither of these Acts has been adequately amended to accommodate developments in these industries. Many of the incentives actually granted exceed the authority of the Acts. In addition incentives are granted for other types of business on an ad hoc basis by executive decision without legislative basis. Apart from the questionable legal enforceability of such incentives they create a culture of expectation and a perception of an unlevel playing field. We recommend strongly that Government regularise the basis for fiscal incentives, that incentives be granted on the basis of statutory authority and policies thereunder which are fully publicised.

The current system does not enable Government to assess or track the value and effectiveness of the incentives it grants. Incentives are Government's contribution to investment and growth and their impact on economic development should be measurable.

PUBLIC/PRIVATE SECTOR RELATIONS

The adoption by Government of the Private Sector Development Strategy, out of which the National Competitiveness Council was established, is a good step. Further action is needed however to create a strong relationship between the public and private sectors without which economic development is constrained and our competitiveness negatively affected.

We recommend in this regard that dialogue between the Government and the private sector representative bodies (particularly the Chamber of Industry and Commerce but also other representative organs of specific service sectors and the professions) be institutionalized to facilitate ongoing official contact and to reduce misunderstandings. There should not be, in a country the size of St. Kitts and Nevis, where contact is so easy, the levels of mistrust and hostility as have existed in the past. It is absolutely essential for the improvement of the competitiveness of St. Kitts and Nevis that there be greater harmony, contact and dialogue between the public and private sectors. This should extend below the level of the political leaders to the top levels of the Civil Service and to all sub sectors within the private sector.

GOVERNMENT TENDERING & PURCHASING

Government is a large consumer of goods and services. By its leverage Government can affect the prospects of individual businesses. It is important therefore that the exercise of these powers, and of Government business generally, be totally transparent in fact and in appearance. We recommended that Government review best practices internationally in this area and introduce legislation to regulate same.

PUBLICATION OF GOVERNMENT POLICIES

Certainty as to Government policy is critical to business stability, efficiency and development. All Government policies which in any way affect or impact on business, industry, investment and entrepreneurship should be published on a Government website.

Given the vast acreage of land owned by Government a clearly enunciated and detailed land use and sale policy should be published on a Government website and in hard copy available at the Government Information Desk. This should include a clear statement of the process to be followed to purchase or lease Government lands and plans of the available areas.

LEGAL SYSTEM

The wheels of the legal system grind too slowly in respect of civil litigation. Justice delayed is often justice denied. The ever increasing criminal activity in the Federation has resulted in the Judges being pre-occupied for much longer than before in presiding over the Criminal Assizes. The time slots set each year for the trial of civil cases are far shorter than they should be. The need for a civil division of the High Court with a Judge dedicated to that work is very evident.

We recommend also that legislation be enacted to allow for attachment of wages to satisfy civil judgments in the High Court and Magistrates Court. This, we are advised, will help to reduce the time of the Courts occupied by proceedings for enforcement of judgments.

We also recommend the early computerization of the official deeds and title records and the separation (as was done with the Companies Registry) of the Registries of Deeds and Titles from the Supreme Court Registry. This will facilitate the more efficient operation of these Registries which contribute to the generation of substantial revenues for Government by way of stamp duties and filing fees.

ENTREPRENEURSHIP

It is worthy of note that St. Kitts and Nevis has the largest number of public companies in the OECS and the largest number of companies listed on the Eastern Caribbean Securities Exchange. The oldest public company on St. Kitts is 50 years old. These companies have a proud record of investment, growth, employment and human resource development. Approximately ten thousand Kittitians and Nevisians are shareholders of the major public companies.

The small and medium size business sectors are also important facets of the service economy which we are developing. The competitiveness of their business and their ability to survive and grow are vital to the competitiveness of the country as a whole.

There has since independence been a steady increase in the number of small and mid size private businesses opened and operating in the Federation. There are still however substantial impediments to the start up and operation of such business enterprises including access to capital, access to training and access to business consultancy. A number of programmes and initiatives have been established in the past few years to address these needs. There appears however to be little co-ordination and rationalization of the efforts of the providers which include the FND, Development Bank, the Credit Union, NEDD and SKIPA. We recommend that a joint public/private sector study be undertaken to assess these programmes and to recommend improved rationalization and effectiveness.

Ways should be sought to expose more students to entrepreneurship skills and opportunities. The Junior Achievement Programme operated through the Chamber of Industry and Commerce and the TDC Warren Tyson Scholarship Programme are sterling examples.

The world is becoming more interconnected. Trade and international agreements will permit foreign owned businesses to move into our country more easily. Our entrepreneurs will face even fiercer competition in future from without. Productivity and excellence of service will be critical factors to the survival of businesses of every size and type. We cannot overstress this fact and use as a simple example the ease with which and extent to which a Chinese owned and operated air-conditioning maintenance service has penetrated the local market despite the existence for over 40 years (through the Technical College) of local training for air-conditioning service and maintenance technicians. What has been lacking in this field has been the high quality of service and the entrepreneurial spirit necessary to convert the training into established businesses. The same could occur in other service and business areas.

It is important also that as a country we recognize the entrepreneurial opportunities available in the growing villa developments on the Southeast Peninsula, Frigate Bay and in other areas of the two islands. These opportunities should be widely promoted through the media and directly to students within the education system.

Street and sidewalk vending have grown out of control. The lack of enforcement and regulation of this informal sector is unacceptable and a disincentive to businesses which follow the law, pay rents and taxes and provide employment. The disorder which this phenomenon encourages is also a danger to peace and good order. There are examples within the region both of the chaos created by this sector and of methods of controlling it. We fully support the stated intention of the Development Control and Planning Board to enforce the law in this area. We urge Government to liaise with the private sector to identify and secure a site for a vendors' market which, if tastefully designed and efficiently planned and built, can enhance the historic town of Basseterre.

ACCESS TO THE DIASPORA AS A MARKET AND RESOURCE BASE

Traditionally, the diaspora has been seen as a source of remittances and bank savings, as overseas votes and as retirees. The diaspora should play a wider and more significant role in the development of our country. We recommend that a more in depth look be taken at the further potential of the diaspora as a market for shares, land, local products and investments and as a resource in services, in tourism and in promotion of our country. For example the many outstanding medical doctors of St. Kitts-Nevis origin in North America should be encouraged to promote investment in medical tourism through contacts with their colleagues. Excellence of the medical services offered is the key to success of this type of venture. Doctors are best placed to identify their fellow professionals with the expertise and interest in this field and to become involved themselves in it.

The large number of highly qualified nationals abroad should also be targeted to contribute their expertise part time at home as do some medical doctors already.

A formal network system should be established to link the diaspora, and organizations within it, with the St. Kitts-Nevis market and the business and arts communities and to promote greater contact and collaboration generally between residents and the diaspora. The system should be designed to foster the development of diaspora networks, beyond the traditional social media contact, to promote interest in areas such as business, the professions, opportunities in higher education and information technology. Exchange visits, conferences and forums should be organized to promote such contact.

We recommend that a data base of the diaspora should be established through the embassies and high commissions working with a local agency involving the public and private sectors. The data base so created should be made available to genuine local entrepreneurs and organizations and used by Government to promote its land sales. We are sure that this direct interest in them will stimulate a patriotic response from the tens of thousands of our nationals in the diaspora and lead to greater interest by successive generations of them in their home country.

Use of the diaspora to promote our tourism product should be enhanced. Greater use should be made of internationally known Kittitians and Nevisians in the promotion of our country abroad. These include Kim Collins, the writer Caryl Phillips, English Premier League footballers Micah Richards and Joleon Lescott, actor/comedian Dexter Felix and the singer Joan Armatrading.

CONCLUSION

In the final analysis as we submit this first report, we are mindful of the fact that there are many other salient points and areas that we could have covered. But given the time frame of the start of The Council, and the urgency to complete this report within the time frame that we set for ourselves, we wanted to put on the agenda the many and varied issues that we have covered. It is our view that as time goes on we would come back to some of these issues with more details, with data and statistical analyses and with other recommendations all geared to making our nation as competitive as it could be from a systemic and systematic point of view. We live in a global society and we have to compete in that global society. But, we have to develop the essential ingredients to operate from an effective, efficient and excellent perspective at home at the same time as we tackle the inevitable external challenges to our competitiveness.

27th May, 2010

RESOLUTION ON CRIME

Escalating violent crime poses a grave and immediate danger to the competitiveness of St. Kitts and Nevis. The trend is likely, if not checked and reversed, to severely damage our economy.

We regard the level of violent crime as a national crisis which requires a national response to re-assert the authority of the State and to address the causes. We find it unhelpful to the resolution of the crisis for it to be politicized. Everyone must be part of the solution. However, the Government and the security forces must lead and be innovative in the fight against crime.

The causes of the crisis are many, varied and well known but worth repeating.

> - Gangs and misguided youth
> - Deportees
> - Easy availability of illegal weapons
> - Limited male role models
> - Children having children
> - Poor parenting
> - Disappearance of "community parenting"
> - Political tribalism
> - Weak law enforcement and crime detection
> - Lack of public confidence in and co-operation with the police
> - Violence on television, the internet, video games and other electronic devices
> - Increased tolerance of violence generally
> - Other negative influences on youth
> - Imported habits
> - Decline in respect for the law
> - Decline in discipline generally
> - Inadequate attention to low achievers in the education system
> - Decline in spiritual pursuits
> - Inhumane prison facilities
> - Lack of correctional facilities for young offenders

There may well be more than the 20 causes listed and these causes are not stated in order of priority.

Many of the causes reflect an endemic decline in attitudes and the growth of negative cultural influences. The responses must target these attitudes and influences and seek to reverse them. Programmes to address some of these causes already exist. With public and financial support for the effective of these programmes and with additional nationally co-ordinated programmes success can be achieved. Such success will be long or at best medium term. We recommend in this regard that Government establish a body including all political parties and the best available representatives of civil society, with full time expert and organizational support, to strategize on a national effort to address the attitudinal and cultural causes of violent crime.

The pressing short term aspect of the solution lies in the physical fight against crime.

This requires:
1. Vastly improved management and equipment of law enforcement.
2. A stronger proactive approach to criminal activity and criminals
3. More effective crime detection
4. Greater deterrence
5. Regional assistance

We are not experts in crime fighting and cannot make direct operational recommendations. We are however capable of assessing and in this case entitled to assess performance and action based on the crime statistics and results of the security forces. On this basis it is irrefutable that current action is failing miserably. As in any enterprise or service, management must take responsibility for the performance of this public service. We urge a new, firmer, more direct and proactive approach from Government and from the security forces.

Index

www.ingramcontent.com/pod-product-compliance
Lightning Source LLC
Chambersburg PA
CBHW050710280326
41926CB00088B/2915